NONE

OF THIS

IS

NORMAL

NONE
OF THIS
IS
NORMAL

THE FICTION OF
JEFF VANDERMEER

BENJAMIN J. ROBERTSON

AFTERWORD BY JEFF VANDERMEER

UNIVERSITY OF MINNESOTA PRESS
MINNEAPOLIS | LONDON

Published by the University of Minnesota Press
111 Third Avenue South, Suite 290
Minneapolis, MN 55401-2520
http://www.upress.umn.edu

ISBN 978-1-5179-0293-3 (pb)
ISBN 978-1-5179-0292-6 (hc)

A Cataloging-in-Publication record for this book is available from the Library of Congress.

Printed in the United States of America on acid-free paper

The University of Minnesota is an equal-opportunity educator and employer.

22 21 20 19 18   10 9 8 7 6 5 4 3 2 1

For Lori

CONTENTS

INTRODUCTION

ALL OF THIS IS NORMAL

Weird fiction's defining feature may well be its refusal to assume any norm. Whereas gothic fictions of the eighteenth, nineteenth, and even twentieth centuries revel in the violation of norms, the weird conveys to its readers the facile or juvenile nature of such transgression: what is transgressed is itself only a human construction built to be so violated. Thus it seems odd to give this book, a book about a writer of (new) weird fiction, the title I have given it. As I shall argue below, the norms violated in Jeff VanderMeer's fiction are not our norms but rather ones that manifest in the fantastic materialities his fictions create and assume. At the same time, however, I cannot help but wonder about the mundane materiality of our own world, the world in which we read these fictions. The past several years have seen the explicit and implicit norms by which we live in the United States and Europe fall on what seems a daily basis. Great Britain's decision to leave the European Union and the presidency of Donald Trump call into question what I have always perceived as normal, especially the need to at least pay lip service to conventional standards of political and social behavior and speech. In the United States, a Republican-controlled Congress has persistently tried to pass legislation of staggering unpopularity. At the same time, people who would surely be hurt by this legislation have cheered it on because it angers those they perceive as their enemies. The executive branch of the American government lies about the potential effects of this legislation, and just about everything else, daily, even as it revises its story about who knew what and when with regard to Russian interventions into the 2016 election. These revisions happen out of sight and out of mind, it seems, because the White House has disallowed recordings of its briefings. The media has made its peace with this revocation of access and simply writes down whatever it is told. The legislative branch has more or less decided that talking to voters is simply too risky, and besides, all of the people who are complaining are from somewhere else and therefore don't deserve any attention. They can't possibly be real, holding the opinions they claim to hold. They must be paid agitators, agents of George Soros, someone who is both all powerful and not able to actually effect any political agenda. Hate crimes and mass shootings now seem a fact of life, a nature beyond the scope of cultural control, and Nazis proudly parade down the street, protected by cops and liberal pundits alike in the name of free speech and honest debate. The Cubs have won a World Series for the first time in living memory.

None of this is normal.

The weird and the new weird, genres with which VanderMeer maintains a complex relationship, have something to teach us: all of this is normal.[1] All of this is normal because all of this is possible. Norms are conventional; they are constructions. This is not to say that they hold no power. Race and gender may be constructions, but they possess tremendous power in every aspect of society and in the day-to-day lives of everyone who lives in society, albeit in uneven, often unjust ways. We ignore such norms at our peril, but ignore them we can, especially if we enjoy the privilege of not being affected by them directly. The weird thus takes for granted not the violation of norms but rather the possibility of other norms—norms that we, as humans bound by inherited logics and patterns of behavior, cannot intuit or inhabit: alien norms, horrifying norms, fantastic norms, weird norms. That there might be other norms—beholden to histories, epistemologies, metaphysics, ontologies, ethics, phenomenologies, aesthetics, or materialities we cannot imagine—provides little comfort when the violation of human norms continues apace with such devastating results. Nonetheless, I hope that a discussion of Jeff VanderMeer's fiction, and by extension the weird and the new weird, as well as how it helps us see possibilities beyond the norms we know, at least makes clear that something else might be possible.

I understand that this is a tall order, perhaps an impossible one, for any book, much less one about a living writer whose complete body of work remains a potentiality rather than a fact. When I began to think about this project, VanderMeer's 2017 novel *Borne* had yet to be released or to receive nearly universal acclaim from scholars such as Wai-Chee Dimock and from the regular book review crowd at the *New Yorker* and the *Los Angeles Review of Books*. By the time *None of This Is Normal* sees publication, the film adaptation of *Annihilation* will have been released, as will, most likely, VanderMeer's next two writing projects: a young adult novel (the first in a trilogy), *Jonathan Lambshead and the Golden Sphere*, and an adult novel, *Hummingbird Salamander*. I am discussing a moving target, a set of texts the final meaning and significance of which will no doubt change as more work appears and new research is undertaken. At the same time, the need to discuss VanderMeer, and to think about what such novels as *Annihilation* and *Borne* might teach us in the present about the present, could not be more urgent. As I argue throughout, VanderMeer's fiction and the worlds he creates authorize modes of thought that help us to interrupt and overcome received wisdom and the entrenched modes of thought that produce this wisdom. In an historical moment when nothing seems normal, and under the conditions of a global catastrophe designated by the Anthropocene invisible to conventional human knowledge practices, any such intervention must be fully investigated and exploited. The lack of scholarship on VanderMeer—as of this writing comprising only two essays, both of which appear in the same volume[2]—makes this matter all the more pressing.

All of this being said, and with this urgency in mind, in the rest of this book, I follow a thread in VanderMeer's fiction having to do with place or location. The various places VanderMeer creates operate according to laws—ontological and epistemological, physical and metaphysical, ethical and moral—quite different than those we assume in our day-to-day lives. As such, these places produce subjects and objects as resistant to our knowledge practices as we can find in contemporary fiction. In pursuit of this end, chapter 1 continues the present discussion of norms by describing more fully how those being violated in VanderMeer's fiction assume different material conditions than those we see violated in our own world. These alien norms are part and parcel of what I call fantastic materiality, a materiality that manifests by way of weird fiction, fantasy, and horror rather than one assumed to be represented or representable in fictions of realist or mimetic leanings. I then define three contexts in which we should think about VanderMeer's fiction and the fantastic materiality it creates: the Anthropocene as an historical period that demands a response from artists and thinkers; the history of weird and new weird fiction, which demonstrates the power of generic hybridity insofar as this hybridity overcomes problems endemic to the codification and reification of fantasy, horror, and science fiction; and what Mark McGurl calls cultural geology, a set of related practices such as speculative realism and new materialism that seeks to overcome anthropocentric and anthropomorphic understandings of the material conditions on which our constructions are built and which we assume in our thought. These contexts provide me with a further opportunity to clarify what I mean by fantastic materiality before I proceed to the body of my argument.

Chapter 2 deals with some of VanderMeer's earliest fictions. These fictions, situated in what VanderMeer calls the Veniss milieu, are organized not by way of a coherent narrative (as in a conventional trilogy or series) but by way of their fragmentary and incoherent production of a milieu around and within a dystopian city called Veniss. This city remains unfixed and unfixable in space and time, even within the context of the fictions set there. As with my discussions of other places in subsequent chapters, my interest in Veniss has to do with how it materializes a world whose conditions challenge anthropocentric and anthropomorphic thought. The Veniss milieu specifically challenges the notion of setting, by which realist and mimeticist fictions limit the time and space in which plot might occur. These limitations must always assume an outside they cannot acknowledge, just as human forms of thought cannot adequately acknowledge or account for the Anthropocene. As a milieu, literally a "middle place," neither between nor among other discrete places and possessing no center of its own, Veniss suggests a form of being beyond that which most fiction "sets." Chapter 3 investigates the Ambergris novels—*City of Saints and Madmen, Shriek: An Afterword,* and *Finch*—and their development of a world whose materiality is its textuality. These novels draw on two seemingly contradictory discourses: first, generic fantasy and its secondary worlds; and second, postmodernist fiction and its excessive textuality. In so doing, the Ambergris novels offer a different fantastic materiality than do the Veniss texts, one in which the text itself provides a ground on which (or, better, a substrate through which) characters can move, a materiality that affords them the power to escape the bottomless and cynical criticality found in prominent examples of postmodernist fiction. Chapter 4 considers VanderMeer's most popular (perhaps) and important (certainly) fiction to date, the Southern Reach trilogy. It demonstrates how Area X, by virtue of borders that do not divide one abstract space from another, suggests a weird planet whose materiality defies human attempts to understand it. The gap between human understanding and the weird planet involves an attitude of abdifference, which flies from both difference and indifference but which nonetheless demands concern for and attention to the weird planet. The geopolitics of the weird planet, as embodied in the encounter of the human with Area X, overcomes a facile liberalism that understands all difference to be amenable to assimilation by virtue of an underlying material condition we always already assume, one that assures sameness by way of homogeneity.

The conclusion turns to VanderMeer's most recent fiction, *Borne,* which stands as one of his most explicitly political statements about climate change to date. VanderMeer understands that any fiction that engages with the relationship of life to what he calls "the broken places," in the postnormal present, participates in a political act. I consider *Borne,* and the related novella *The Strange Bird: A Borne Story,* in the context of life in the broken places as suggesting "life after aftermath," not so much a representation of what human life will look like in a postapocalyptic world as a fantasizing of what comes after both the human and the anthropomorphic, anthropocentric notion of aftermath itself. Aftermath suggests, in the argument of John Clute, problem without solution. Life after aftermath is a form of life for which there is no need of solution because there is no problem. For this life, the broken places are not broken. They are the material condition of this life and therefore whole to this life. For the human, such a wholeness can only ever be part and parcel of fantasy; it can never involve a reality whose truth only reveals itself through the knowledge practices that produced the broken places to begin with.

Ultimately I cannot pretend to have provided here a complete account of VanderMeer's career, or even a comprehensive reading of the several worlds he creates in his major fictions. Nonetheless, I hope that in this book I can make visible some of the major themes and concerns within that fiction, as well as provide a means by which to grasp its importance to our postnormal world.

1

AMBERGRIS RULES

GENRE AND MATERIALITY
IN THE ANTHROPOCENE

There is no distant place anymore. And along with distance,
objectivity is gone as well, or at least an older notion of objectivity
that was unable to take into account the active subject of history.
—Bruno Latour, "Agency at the Time of the Anthropocene"

AMBERGRIS RULES

Finch (2009), the final installment in Jeff VanderMeer's Ambergris trilogy, begins like so many detective novels have begun before: dead bodies, and a man who must make sense of them. If *Finch* were an early example of the detective genre, it would describe a brilliant mind's attempt to bring an abnormal situation into accord with a social or legal norm, to narrativize the bodies' deaths in order to produce justice—or at the very least eliminate a threat to the world. If it were a later example, one of the hard-boiled variety, it would recognize that social or legal norms no longer hold, if indeed they ever had. The detective would therefore adhere to a personal, perhaps idiosyncratic code of conduct in the face of chaos. Solving the crime would not redeem the lawless world, but the detective could nonetheless save some small part of it, often the part with which he was involved, according to his understanding of the way things ought to be. If *Finch* belonged to an increasingly nihilistic late noir, then the detective would no longer maintain even a nominal relationship to social norms or a personal code. He would meet the world on its own terms, using any weapon to hand and abandoning rules that would constrain him in his mission to stop others from doing the same. His very acts of investigation would doubtless contribute to the chaos detectives were formerly tasked with holding at bay. Such recursion cannot be helped in a world whose fallenness is not only visible and obvious but also constitutive and ontological. Whatever instance of the detective genre we examine, it will assume some norm, be it one that must be defended and reproduced, one that has been lost but remains aspirational, or one that can only be understood as a myth best forgotten in the face of an ongoing war of all against all. Such norms in turn assume the world, this world, the primary world, the world whose materiality provides a ground on which norms can be inhabited, constructed, questioned, and debunked. When in this world we encounter a norm of any sort, we encounter it according to patterns and modes of thought conditioned by this materiality. We encounter it both as something that derives from this materiality and as something that can be apprehended and comprehended according to intellectual techniques that likewise derive from this materiality.

How does this entanglement of materiality, subjectivity, situation, and norms operate when the first term in this list is wholly other—when it is a separate or secondary materiality, a fantastic materiality?

When John Finch arrives on the scene to investigate a double murder, enjoined to do so by a message that "was already dying in his hand" on his arrival, he discovers that one of the bodies has been cut in half by unknown means.[1] The body is not human but that of a *fanaarcensitii*, or gray cap—one of Ambergris's fungal rulers—and only its torso and head are present. The other body is that of a man with a beard that seems to be made of fungus, but "that wasn't unusual."[2] Both bodies appear to have fallen from a great height, although they are found in a structurally sound apartment with regular, apartment-appropriate dimensions.

Finch's boss, another gray cap with a name Finch can only render as Heretic, supervises the investigation on the scene even though Finch arrives during the day and the gray caps rarely leave their underground city except at night, when it is dark and fungus can spread unchallenged. A Partial, a human whose fungal infiltration makes him a living camera and grants him ecstatic visions, takes pictures of the scene and guards the bodies when Heretic departs and leaves the case to Finch. Finch seems to have a past that he would prefer to remain unknown to most of his associates, including the Partial, although Heretic knows of it and does not care. These are only the fifth and sixth murder victims Finch has been called on to investigate during his time as a detective, a position he has taken in the wake of the gray caps' Rising from their underground world in the aftermath of a destructive civil war among the houses that constitute the sum total of Ambergris's economy, to take over the city for reasons that remain mysterious. Of the first four murder investigations, only one revealed an actual murder, and that one was solved in a single day. This one seems different. When Finch asks Heretic whether the gray cap body's lack of blood is normal, Heretic responds: "No, it's not normal." Unprovoked and unacknowledged, the Partial adds, "None of this is normal."[3]

This scene is crucial to the overall plot of *Finch*. However, it also offers a way into Jeff VanderMeer's fictions and the worlds they create; it provides a means to grasp how these worlds are different than our own and how this difference produces assumptions and knowledge practices altogether uninhabitable by anthropomorphic and anthropocentric thought. To a reader situated in the primary world—this world, earth—the Partial's statement rings true. That reader may know detective fiction, but *Finch* is not simply detective fiction (although it is also that). *Finch* describes an alien situation, wholly unknown and perhaps unknowable to the reader—a familiar feeling to anyone who has spent any time with science fiction, fantasy, or horror. However, the Partial's statement points to something more than a disjunction between the primary world where the reader reads and the secondary world in which Ambergris exists. It points to norms of and from that world, be they real or mythical, natural or constructed—norms that cannot be the reader's norms insofar as they manifest among subjects and in situations deter-mined by a materiality that the reader cannot know. It points to a fan-tastic materiality. Finch's presence at this murder scene is not normal. He does not investigate many murders, certainly not ones this unusual. Heretic's presence is likewise not normal: neither he nor any other gray cap appears above ground in Ambergris during the day except in the most unusual, and often horrifying, circumstances. The Partial's pres-ence may be normal, but his affect and attitude are not: he contradicts Heretic and seems to have his own agenda, which may be in conflict not only with the human Finch (on whom the Partial looks down as unev-olved and therefore unenlightened) but also with the gray caps, who granted to the Partial all of his powers. The state of the two bodies is far from normal, as is the fact that they are found together; humans and gray caps do not willingly mix company. The state of Ambergris as a whole, destroyed both by the conventional weapons of human war and by the fungal bombs and infections loosed by the gray caps, is far from normal, even in the context of this world.

Nothing in this situation accords with any law. Finch thus might attempt to interpret the situation and solve the case to make things right, to realign the world with itself. He might seek to bring the world into accord with social norms or statutory law—or, in the absence of such, his personal code. If the world is too fallen, if the situation is indicative of a constitutive chaos, then perhaps Finch might engage in a war of all against all, fighting not for the law but for survival and to protect what he cares about. Yet such a fight assumes norms—absent, lost, or con-structed ones—against which chaos can be judged. These norms, how-ever, cannot be our norms. Finch cannot fix his world according to the rules that govern ours. He must make his own history according to what he inherits, and the history he inherits has its own metaphysics because it rests on its own physics. Finch lives by "Ambergris rules."[4]

Finch cannot be read as paradigmatic of Jeff VanderMeer's fiction. Although I demonstrate throughout this book that VanderMeer's fiction shares a concern with what I call fantastic materiality, the individual texts and groups of texts that make up this body of work do not develop this concern in the same fashion. Nonetheless, I focus on VanderMeer's fiction, mainly the novels (excluding much of his other writing in the service of a clear argument). VanderMeer's fictional worlds manifest materialities that do not represent the given reality that realist, mimetic, historicist, and critical fictions assume even as they question it. I offer a limited view of Jeff VanderMeer, but I do so with a specific intent: to show how fantastic materialities hint at other ways of thinking about our own world at a moment in history when so much of human thought, to the extent that it remains conditioned by modern ideals and techniques, seems to fail. Rather than embracing this horror, as so many generic and theoretical responses to this historical moment seem to do, VanderMeer's fiction suggests that there may be other ways to proceed.

The fiction I address here represents only a fraction of VanderMeer's contributions to contemporary cultural production. He has only become well known to mainstream audiences in the past several years, after the 2014 publication of the Southern Reach trilogy in Farrar, Straus & Giroux's then recently established FSG Originals line of paperbacks. However, his career as a writer began in the late 1980s. His career as an editor extends nearly as far back, and before the success of the Southern Reach trilogy, he may have been as well known for his work shaping the landscape of genre fiction since the mid-1990s as he was for his fiction. Aside from novels, VanderMeer has published dozens of short stories in various periodicals, as chapbooks, and in collected editions. He has published poetry, flash fiction, and essays. He has written a movie tie-in novel: *Predator: South China Sea* (2008). He has written books of advice for aspiring writers, both of the earnest and straightforward sort (*Booklife: Strategies and Survival Tips for the 21st-Century Writer*, 2009) and of an equally earnest but more whimsical variety (*Wonderbook: The Illustrated Guide to Creating Imaginative Fiction*, 2013, and *The Steampunk User's Manual: An Illustrated Practical and Whimsical Guide to Creating Retro-Futurist Dreams*, 2014). He has edited with his wife, Ann VanderMeer (formerly Ann Kennedy), definitive collections of contemporary genre fiction: *The New Weird* (2008), *The Weird: A Compendium of Strange and Dark Stories* (2011), *Sisters of the Revolution: A Feminist Speculative Fiction Anthology* (2015), and *The Big Book of Science Fiction: The Ultimate Collection* (2016). On his own and with his wife, he has also edited numerous other collections of fantastika, including volumes of yearly bests and volumes of cutting-edge, genre-bending fiction.[5] Then there are the truly strange texts, such as *The Thackery T. Lambshead Guide to Eccentric and Discredited Diseases* (2003), *The Kosher Guide to Imaginary Animals* (2010), and *The Thackery T. Lambshead Cabinet of Curiosities* (2011). This list of VanderMeer's works, both in terms of its size and its variety, suggests a difficult task for any critic. Making this task even more difficult is the fact that VanderMeer's writing often appears in multiple editions, some of which have been limited and thus are hard to come by. His stories and fragments have, for example, appeared in chapbooks before appearing in collections or as sections of novels. Some work, such as *City of Saints and Madmen* (2001–4) and the short story collection *Secret Life* (2004, revised as *Secret Life: The Select Fire Remix* in 2006), appears in multiple editions, revised and remixed with each new iteration. *Finch* itself appeared not only as a standard-issue trade paperback but also in several special editions, which variously included in-world ephemera and the novel's official soundtrack.

Although VanderMeer's career has unfolded in our own world, it seems to adhere to no familiar law. In my attempts to navigate the complexity of his corpus, I have often felt like Shadrach, Duncan Shriek, or the biologist—characters in VanderMeer's fiction who leave the daylight behind and proceed underground to discover not just complexity but a complexity beholden to laws altogether different than the ones assumed in day-to-day life. These characters do not emerge from their undergrounds as the selves they were before they entered, although what they are different than on that emergence remains a mystery. I have found it necessary in this study of VanderMeer's work to simplify this complexity in the interests of clarity, brevity, and argument. I am not sure that VanderMeer's career can be adequately addressed by a single argument, so I have addressed a small thread that runs through a large and complex whole. Thus I largely set aside his editorial work, poetry, movie tie-ins, nonfiction, and oddities. I do not spend much time on the short fiction except where its settings or characters intersect with those of the novels. I hope this focus provides clarity with regard to a specific contribution VanderMeer makes to contemporary thought.

For the remainder of this chapter, I present three contexts in and by which we might understand VanderMeer's fiction: an historical context (the Anthropocene), a generic context (the weird and the new weird), and a critical context (what Mark McGurl calls the new cultural geology). These contexts overlap and engage with one another. The Anthropocene binds together much that was once assumed to be separate. As a genre, the new weird also binds together things once assumed to be separate (e.g., science fiction with horror, fantasy with science fiction) and has a periodization that roughly coincides with the popularization of the Anthropocene as a concept and term. Both the Anthropocene and the new weird suggest and influence cultural geology, a theoretical preoccupation dedicated to describing newly understood human entanglements with the planet on which the human stands. Cultural geology, by rethinking and undermining modern knowledge practices, in turn helps render the Anthropocene visible as a human concern at inhuman scales and reveals how (new) weird fiction grapples with such scales. Similar to cultural geology, the new weird concerns itself with the entanglements of subjects with their material conditions, even if these material conditions are fantastic. Although I must treat these contexts consecutively, they attach to one another in innumerable productive ways. In the chapters that follow, I expand on and complicate the issues I raise in these discussions, especially insofar as VanderMeer's fiction does not simply embody any of them. Finally, in the last section of this chapter, I turn to the notion of fantastic materiality. Materiality is the opposite of fantastic; it is the stuff of objective reality itself, that which makes everything else possible. Even if we acknowledge that VanderMeer or other writers and artists might represent an alien materiality, we must nonetheless acknowledge that they produce it by virtue of the actual materiality under which they work. Thus any so-called fantastic materiality must be understood as bound by the logics of this one. All of this is true. I do not present fantastic materiality here as something floating free of history, as a true metaphysics or transcendental concept. Rather, it is a concept in part determined by the contexts in which it appears and by the other concepts with which it engages. Nonetheless, it renders possible thought that we might not otherwise think, especially when we understand that its power lies not in its representational or critical capacities but in its affective and material ones.

THE ANTHROPOCENE

Although "Anthropocene" has come to be associated with catastrophic climate change and other environmental crises, popularized by way of a short essay by Nobel laureate Paul Crutzen in 2002, the term refers to a proposed geologic epoch that would follow from the Holocene.[6] This epoch begins, according to various accounts, in the late eighteenth century, with the advent of the use of fossil fuels; in the mid-twentieth century, with the use of nuclear weapons at the end of the World War II and the subsequent development of nuclear power; or at the dawn of human agriculture roughly 10,000 years ago, which would make it congruent with the Holocene. Despite more recent usage that broadens its scope, the term was coined to make visible a geologic epoch characterized by the fossilization of human activity in the geologic record.[7] Fossil fuels have stored the sun's energy in the earth's crust for hundreds of millions of years. Their consumption, and related human actions, has released this energy in the span of mere centuries. The release of so much energy in such a short period of time—on a geologic scale, even the 10,000-year period that makes up the Holocene is nearly nothing— has imprinted itself in stone and radically destabilized the ground on which humans walk—conditions that allow for their continued existence and that of their civilizations.

As a context for the present argument, the Anthropocene provides a periodizing concept for VanderMeer's fiction more than it does an explicit theme. VanderMeer clearly thematizes environmental issues in some of the Veniss texts, in *Shriek: An Afterword* (2006), *Finch*, the Southern Reach trilogy (enticing one reviewer to call him "the weird Thoreau"[8]), and *Borne* (2017). VanderMeer has written about the Anthropocene and some of its theoretical elaborations in the wake of the success of the Southern Reach trilogy and has engaged in productive dialogue with scholars of the concept.[9] However, VanderMeer's representation of environmental collapse and the human reaction to it is of less interest to me than the glimpses his fiction offers of materialities and their attendant knowledge practices outside of the modern ones that in part caused the Anthropocene. Given my argument that VanderMeer's worlds must be understood in and of themselves, irreducible to and nondeducible from the reader's world, I cannot claim that any environmental concerns found in his fiction allegorize or historicize the Anthropocene by symbolic encoding. I am not interested here in whether VanderMeer writes about the Anthropocene, even if he does in fact do so. Rather, I am interested in the fact that he writes during the Anthropocene, both the epoch itself but more importantly the period of our awareness of the epoch. Although the former issue remains a valid one, a consideration of the material conditions under which VanderMeer has written and to which his writing contributes is far more important than the question of representation because such material conditions demand and produce new forms of human thought.

My designation of the Anthropocene as an historical context warrants further explanation, especially insofar as the Anthropocene may appear at first glance and in a simplified sense to be ahistorical—a natural event, perhaps. Even if we recognize that the Anthropocene constitutively involves both nature and the human, it remains an event whose temporal and spatial dimensions so outstrip what we normally call "the historical" that it cannot be related to this humanistic framework; nor can it be made to mean anything to human subjects.[10] If nothing else, the Anthropocene forces the human subject to confront finitude: the brevity of temporal existence, the boundaries of spatial existence, and the meaninglessness of the narratives produced under such brevity and within such boundaries. The Anthropocene stands opposed to history, the time of human being and the framework in which human meaning accrues. In this confrontation of one with the other, the human becomes radically dislodged from its familiar and comfortable position as the subject of a narrative called history, from its role as the protagonist in the drama called Man. (This narrative is all too often masculinist as well as colonialist, racist, and classist.) However, humanity, in its disappointed state, cannot retreat to nature, which can nowhere be found after human action has transformed the very earth itself. A brief discussion of these

two separate spheres—history and nature—in terms of certain understandings of their respective endings will clarify this point.

Around the time VanderMeer was getting his start as a writer, both
history and nature—each long considered enduring, even eternal—
ended. In a much-debated essay, Francis Fukuyama declared that with
the collapse of actually existing communism in the late 1980s, democratic liberalism reigned supreme. In the absence of an ideological other
for this political and economic system, history, "as understood as a single,
coherent, evolutionary process, when taking into account the experience
of all people in all times," had come to an end.[11] At the same time that this
end was coming about, Bill McKibben declared another: that of nature.
Although scientific consensus implied that natural events take place
in geologic time—over the course of hundreds of millions of years—
McKibben understood this truth to mask another, less comfortable one:
human civilization, despite its relatively short duration, had materially
affected the earth's atmosphere. With that, no part of the world could
anymore be called pristine or untouched by human hand or action; the
recognition of such signifies the end of nature.

Each of these endings had less to do with any new material cataclysm than with a proposed shift in human perception and language.
Yes, the world order was shaken when communism ended, but things
still happened. These things could simply no longer be understood to be
part and parcel of progress, of a larger project called history according
to which humanity sought, intentionally or otherwise, to produce the
best possible world for itself. Fukuyama puts it this way: "This is not to
say that there will no longer be events to fill the pages of *Foreign Affairs's*
yearly summaries of international relations, for the victory of liberalism
has occurred primarily in the realm of ideas or consciousness and is as
yet incomplete in the real or material world."[12] For McKibben, after the
end of nature, there would still be trees, animals, oceans, and mountains, but such entities, individually or collectively, could no longer
simply stand vis-à-vis the human as its other. The human had become
inextricably involved with them when it intervened into their bodies and
systems by way of its acquisition of natural resources and its production,
consumption, and distribution of consumer goods derived from such

resources. As McKibben puts it, "By the end of nature I do not mean the end of the world. The rain will still fall and the sun shine, though differently than before. When I say 'nature,' I mean a certain set of human ideas about the world and our place in it."[13]

As a periodizing concept, the Anthropocene draws together these two endings, too often understood separately. It does so not in the name of an imminent cataclysm, although it recognizes that such a cataclysm may well be imminent. Rather, it makes clear the extent to which the separation of the spheres of history and nature, as well as their articulations as human ideals, have brought the planet to the brink of this cataclysm. History and nature, according to certain understandings of each, came to an end around 1989. With the birth of the Anthropocene, we witness the reemergence of both. This reemergence is characterized by a fundamental entanglement of these conceptually separated spheres with one another. History in the manner understood by Fukuyama (by way of Hegel and Alexandre Kojève) largely excludes nature. Nature is the given against which the subject struggles in order to produce meaning, but that given is nowhere to be found apart from its interaction with the human. Nature only ever becomes historical insofar as it means something for the human. Likewise, as McKibben's discussion of nature implies, the natural world ceases to be natural when it is corrupted by human presence (or the presence of some human proxy, such as solid, liquid, or gaseous pollution). History overcomes and eliminates nature as a necessary consequence of its processes. In each case, the spheres exclude each other. There can be no nonhuman nature within the context of history; nature disappears in the presence of human encroachment and the valorization of the given world.

Such criticality, which always already understands the human and nature to remain separate, cannot hold in the Anthropocene, and our new awareness of a challenge to not just this or that old notion but also to the deeper assumptions that ground our thought, registers the Anthropocene as a periodizing concept. During this period, the human and the earth intimately attach to and involve one another. This attachment and involvement, always already material and lived, and now also conceptual and known, force us to confront questions about what it means to be human, how human meaning is produced, and what the grounds for human action and thought are. Two related examples of this confrontation between human knowledge and the natural world serve to illustrate this point. First, Dipesh Chakrabarty notes,

> Climate scientists raise a problem of scale for the human imagination, though they do not usually think through the humanistic implications of their own claim that, unlike the changes in climate this planet has seen in the past, the current warming is anthropogenic in nature. Humans, collectively, now have an agency in determining the climate of the planet as a whole, a privilege reserved in the past only for very large-scale geophysical forces.[14]

That human beings have a "species being" has been long claimed, if not always accepted.[15] That humans act as a species, and at scales almost entirely imperceptible to individual humans or the species itself, is only newly recognized.

We cannot, however, name and describe this collective activity, what the human does as a species, according to preexisting human knowledge practices, whether scientific and objective or sociopolitical and subjective. How does one study the interaction of more than seven billion people and the ground on which they stand? How does one ascribe moral responsibility for the planet's condition to an entire species, especially given the radically different conditions under which segments of that species operate? How can we even speak of a species such as humanity without addressing the manner in which such classifications have been wielded by authorities to dehumanize so many individuals and groups throughout history? As Chakrabarty knows, humanity is far less responsible for the Anthropocene than is the West or the overdeveloped world or even capitalism. Asking humanity to solve this problem when humanity is so fraught and its myriad components so variously (un)empowered seems to be a fool's errand. Yet the Anthropocene asks that we do exactly this.

Where Chakrabarty describes how a collective action imperceptible to individuals or even groups entangles human subjects with one
another, Timothy Clark demonstrates why humanity must begin to
think at an altogether different scale: that of the planet as a whole. Clark
also addresses the challenge to modern forms of thought that this new
scale presents. The Anthropocene redefines what we understand to be
the ground on which subjects act and on which history takes place by
demanding that we take that ground as an object and thereby reduce it
to a scale at which objects can mean for and to us. Scale is relative—
and, more importantly, nonneutral. The very existence of an historical or natural event, the human capacity to perceive it and to name it,
depends on the scale at which it takes place. Clark writes, "We inhabit
distance, height and breadth in terms of the given dimensionality of our
embodied, earthly existence. This particular physical scale is inherent to
the intelligibility of things around us, imbued with an obviousness and
authority which it takes an effort to override."[16] Nonetheless, the difficulty our embodied instruments introduce to our efforts to measure
climate change and the effects of human action on the geologic record
are only part of the problem—and perhaps are the easiest part to solve.
Overcoming the obviousness of human-perceptible scales, spatially and
temporally, may be difficult, but it can be done.

The greater difficulty lies elsewhere—namely in the fact that once
we think at planetary scales, according to geologic or cosmological
time, we must suddenly ask where we are standing and when we are
standing there. How do we think of nearly the whole of human civilization as well as its material conditions when the very possibility of
such thought depends on the thing we are trying to think, namely the
material earth itself? With regard to Carl Sagan's discussion of the "pale
blue dot" photograph of the earth taken by the *Voyager 1* space probe
in 1990, Clark writes:

> This is the planet of the human archive, support of
> all cultural memory, the fragile material matrix of all
> inscription, self-relation, commemoration. Again, the earth

is read solely as an index of the human . . . , but one now
collapsed towards an impossible experience of overload, to
be forced to imagine almost everything about human life all
at once and in the one site—the myriad incommensurable
horizons shrinking down upon each other like a point, like
water down a plughole.[17]

Of course, with very few exceptions, human beings remain standing on
earth even as they contemplate the earth itself. In the Anthropocene,
however, we must think about humanity as it so stands and think about
what it stands on. We must also think of these two entities together
insofar as they mutually constitute one another and through the trans-
formations that such constitution involves.

The Anthropocene does not replace one stable condition, such as
nature or the earth, with another. It reveals a process of give and take
between entities that exist at very different scales, and it thus requires
us to ask what forms of thought suffice to address, imagine, or transform
it. Bruno Latour makes a point similar to Clark's when he notes that the
earth in the Anthropocene takes on an agency of its own and becomes
an actor, thus hinting at its role in a drama rather than the stage on
which a drama is set.[18] The intervention of the earth into human affairs,
the result of a complex process that includes conscious and unconscious
human intervention into earthly affairs, renders many of our most cher-
ished and ingrained intellectual techniques invalid:

I think it is easy for us to agree that, in modernism, people
are not equipped with the mental and emotional repertoire
to deal with such a vast scale of events; that they have
difficulty submitting to such a rapid acceleration for which, in
addition, they are supposed to feel responsible while, in the
meantime, this call for action has none of the traits of their
older revolutionary dreams. How can we simultaneously be
part of such a long history, have such an important influence,
and yet be so late in realizing what has happened and so utterly
impotent in our attempts to fix it?[19]

Scholars have attempted to address this complex state of affairs, first by recognizing that the Anthropocene requires thought that escapes from the thought we inherit from modernity, and second by endeavoring to produce such new forms. Two thinkers of the Anthropocene and the politics of knowledge in the contemporary world, Donna Haraway and McKenzie Wark, offer examples. Following specifically from Latour, among others, Haraway theorizes SF as a method of creating narratives for the Anthropocene. SF refers not only to science fiction but also to "speculative fabulation, speculative feminism, science fact, so far."[20] SF draws together heterogeneous entities—humans, institutions, animals, technologies, cultural and ethnic groups, genders, sexual orientations, racialized identities—in order to disrupt dominant narratives of progress. Wark calls for "low theory," a concept he borrows from Jack Halberstam: "Rather than imagining theory as a policing faculty flying high as a drone over all the others, a low theory is interstitial, its labor communicative rather than controlling."[21] Like Haraway, Wark's answer to the Anthropocene involves finding connections among seemingly unlike entities and allowing these entities to express themselves through this discovery, rather than insisting on abstract, a priori connections dictated in the name of proper understanding. Haraway and Wark, along with many other thinkers in the humanities and social sciences,[22] thus imagine history and nature together, inseparable from and constitutive of one another. In the period when this entanglement not only can be thought but must be thought, VanderMeer's fiction develops a means by which to do so.

THE NEW WEIRD AND THE WEIRD

An historical period characterized by a need to recognize and understand the entanglement among entities conventionally understood to be radically distinct from one another requires and deserves a genre and a critical methodology predicated on admixture and hybridity. I turn my attention to such a critical methodology in the following section. Here I introduce the generic categories of the weird and the new weird. VanderMeer's fiction cannot be reduced to any generic framework, even ones as fluid and (at times) incoherent as those provided by the weird and the new weird. Nonetheless, the following discussion makes clear how these genres—by way of their historical situations as well as their formal, philosophical, and political preoccupations—offer insight into VanderMeer's project and the particular works it comprises.

VanderMeer has been associated with the new weird, however it is defined, at least since science fiction and fantasy writer (and new weird inspiration) M. John Harrison coined the term in 2003. Harrison addressed the following provocation to his Third Alternative Message Board: "The New Weird. Who does it? What is it? Is it even anything? Is it even New? Is it, as some think, not only a better slogan than The Next Wave, but also incalculably more fun to do? Should we just call it Pick'n'Mix instead? As ever, *your* views are the views I want to hear."[23] Responses to Harrison consistently refer to two writers as practitioners of the new weird: VanderMeer for *City of Saints and Madmen* and China Miéville for *Perdido Street Station* (2000), perhaps the ur-text of the new weird for the discussion that unfolded on Harrison's board. (Both VanderMeer and Miéville were participants in the discussion, as was Steph Swainston, who would become central to the new weird for *The Year of Our War*, published within a year of when this discussion began, in 2004.)

The various threads that developed in response to Harrison's prompt are nearly impossible to summarize, perhaps because, as several participants argue, the new weird itself is such a slippery concept. Indeed, several participants disdain the term for being a crass marketing ploy or mere slogan. Others reject it for the fact that it calls attention to, and thus potentially ruins, something that should not be given over to popular, public consciousness. Still others state that the new weird is not in fact new, and that writers such as Clive Barker worked in the genre in the 1980s. Despite these arguments, or perhaps as a result of them, two important and related points arise from this discussion. First, the term "new weird" consciously refers back to the weird fiction published in *Weird Tales*, a pulp periodical whose heyday ran from 1923 to 1938, especially in terms of the genre fluidity that characterizes the period and the periodical, at least in retrospect. According to one commenter, the new weird recalls "a pre-generic pulp era where [science fiction], fantasy and horror were less well defined." As Harrison put it, in response to this claim, "[The new weird] makes that exact allusion to *Weird Tales* and especially the fact that, back then, in that marvellous & uncorrupted time of the world, everything could still be all mixed up together— horror, sf, fantasy—and no one told you off or said your career was over with their firm if you kept doing that."[24]

Second, the new weird, especially for Steph Swainston, rejects Tolkienesque fantasy:

> The New Weird is a kickback against jaded heroic fantasy which has been the only staple for too long. Instead of stemming from Tolkien, it is influenced by [Mervyn Peake's] *Gormenghast* and [M. John Harrison's] *Viriconium*. It is incredibly eclectic, and takes ideas from anywhere. It borrows from American Indian and Far Eastern mythology rather than European or Norse traditions, but the main influence is modern culture—street culture—mixing with ancient mythologies. The text isn't experimental, but the creatures are. It is amazingly empathic. What is it like to be a clone? Or to walk on your hundred quirky legs? The New Weird attempts to explain. It acknowledges other literary traditions, for example [Angela] Carter's mainstream fiction, or classics like [Herman] Melville. Films are a source of inspiration because action is vital. The elves were the first against the wall when the revolution came, and instead we want the vastness of the science fiction film universe on the page.[25]

Insofar as it recalls a period in which genre codification had not yet limited writers to this or that set of conventions, structures, and themes, and insofar as it rejects at least one of the major codifications of fantastika (the Tolkienesque heroic fantasy), the new weird involves a reentanglement and reimagining of extant forms. In a 2003 essay, VanderMeer describes what was then sometimes called interstitial fiction in similar terms: "For a long time now, a sea change has been occurring in the world of fiction. Cross-pollination has, more and more, become an element of the best fiction."[26] Although in a note to this essay added in 2004 he largely disavows categorizing schemes, VanderMeer nonetheless demonstrates enthusiasm for fiction that challenges rigid formulation. In any case, the new weird and its related forms draw on what has come before, but it defines what has come before according to new standards that exclude certain obvious antecedents while drawing attention to others that are less commonly known. It pays homage to the past, but it does so by way of an insistence on its own novelty (albeit a novelty often knowing to the point of irony).

All such claims notwithstanding, the new weird remains a difficult term and movement to define. It seems to have at least two major points of origin: the period between 1999 and 2003 bookended by the Seattle World Trade Organization protests and Harrison's question cited above (in the midst of which *Perdido Street Station* was published); and the 1980s, when writers such as Clive Barker and Thomas Ligotti and filmmakers such as David Cronenberg produced some of their most important and groundbreaking work.[27] To make sense of these periodizations and of the importance of the new weird as a context for VanderMeer's fiction, I wish to compare it briefly to the weird along three closely related lines: by way of its hybridization of generic structures and conventions, by way of how its monsters imply a worldview or politics, and by way of the worlds in which it is set.

S. T. Joshi argues that the weird cannot be understood as an organic or authentic genre and that its status as a genre has only been established after the fact by fans and scholars. The most prominent of the first wave of weird writers, who in Joshi's periodization produced their major work between 1880 and 1940, did not understand themselves to be working within generic constraints or according to generic conventions. Likewise, they often worked in ignorance of one another.[28] Only after H. P. Lovecraft's important 1927 essay, "Supernatural Horror in Literature," grouped together Arthur Machen, Algernon Blackwood, Lord Dunsany, and M. R. James as modern masters of horror, in a line with but distinct from the gothic writers of the eighteenth and nineteenth centuries, did weird fiction come to possess something like a generic identity.[29] Nonetheless, the weird's lack of generic boundaries has not stopped readers, such as the commenter cited above, from finding in it nascent aspects of genres that would come to dominate the popular fiction landscape in the second half of the twentieth century: fantasy, science fiction, and horror. As China Miéville puts it, "If considered at all, Weird Fiction is usually, roughly, conceived of as a rather breathless and generically slippery macabre fiction, a dark fantastic ('horror' plus 'fantasy') often featuring nontraditional alien monsters (thus plus 'science fiction')."[30] Of course, our recognition of contemporary genre structures and conventions in the weird must be understood as anachronistic. We might trace horror back to Horace Walpole and Ann Radcliffe, science fiction back to Jules Verne and H. G. Wells, and fantasy back to William Morris and Andrew Lang. However, none of these genres was understood as a genre until the first decades of the twentieth century at the earliest, in part because periodicals such as *Weird Tales* devoted themselves to the dissemination and codification of these genres. At the very least, we should pause before understanding Lovecraft, Clark Ashton Smith, or Robert Howard to have consciously drawn on a well-defined set of structures or conventions as they produced their fictions.

In contrast, new weird writers such as VanderMeer, Miéville, Swainston, K. J. Bishop, and Felix Gilman consciously draw on well-understood generic structures and conventions to achieve startling results. Miéville has explicitly stated that he "revels" in genre, often to the detriment of fictional devices such as "character" and "plot."[31] He has also written about the limitations of science fiction vis-à-vis fantasy and embodied his argument in his fiction.[32] Swainston draws on fantasy as well as science fiction and horror in her Castle novels, in which hordes of interdimensional insects ravage a world protected by a group of immortals more interested in maintaining their own power than they are in finishing the war they are tasked with prosecuting.[33] Bishop and Gilman, to different degrees, draw on not only genres of the fantastic but also the western. Bishop does so to think about the nature of art and belief, and Gilman to think about the conceptual underpinnings of American manifest destiny and the genocide it authorizes.[34] These admixtures of genre, however, are quite different than what we find in the weird proper, if for no other reason than they are produced knowingly and in reaction to the rigid distinctions that rendered individual genres stale and made remixing necessary in the first place. In each case, however, the new weird makes clear the artificiality of such distinctions (which remain real nonetheless), as well as the importance of thinking with and through entanglement. Science fiction, fantasy, and horror (and the western and detective fiction) each have inherent limits. Science fiction tends to think historically and fantasy ahistorically, for example. Their juxtaposition in Miéville's *The Scar* (2002) not only makes those limitations clear but also produces new ways of thinking that move beyond them.

One of the ways in which the new weird moves beyond certain genre constraints is through its monsters and the worldview and politics these monsters imply. Lovecraft noted how the monsters in M. R. James's "ghost stories" must be distinguished from the disembodied spirits found in other examples of the form: "The average James host is lean, dwarfish, and hairy—a sluggish, hellish night-abomination halfway betwixt beast and man—and usually *touched* before *seen*."[35] Miéville develops this line of thought when he argues that the weird's "break with previous fantastics is vividly clear in its teratology, which renounces all folkloric or traditional antecedents. The monsters of high Weird are indescribable and formless . . . and their constituent bodyparts are disproportionately insectile/cephalopodic, without mythic resonance."[36] The shift to the weird monster from more traditional forms of monstrosity, such as those found in the gothic, signals another shift, namely to a weird ontology: "[H. P. Lovecraft's] Great Old Ones (Outer Monstrosities, in [William Hope] Hodgson's formulation) neither haunt nor linger. The Weird is not the return of any repressed: though always described as ancient, and half-recalled by characters from spurious texts, this recruitment to invented cultural memory does not avail Weird monsters of Gothic's strategy of revenance, but back-projects their radical unremembered alterity into history, to en-Weird ontology itself."[37]

This weird ontology, and the antihumanistic, materialistic worldview it suggests, has done much to drive interest in the philosophical and theoretical modes of thought I discuss below, largely as a result of the elevation of Lovecraft to nigh canonical status for scholars interested in such matters. Mark McGurl refers to Lovecraft as part of what he calls "the posthuman comedy," despite his former relegation to the status of merely generic pulp.[38] Graham Harman, one of the most prominent practitioners of and proponents for object-oriented ontology, has claimed Lovecraft as a muse for his philosophy in the manner that Friedrich Hölderlin was for Heidegger.[39] Although they do not mention the Anthropocene by name, Carl H. Sederholm and Jeffrey Andrew Weinstock explain recent scholarly attention to Lovecraft by way of his antihumanism and what it reveals about human finitude: "What his fiction tells us is that, however grand we consider human accomplishment, it will all inevitably disappear into the unplumbable depths of time. Put another way, Lovecraft's significance to key philosophical debates rests on his assertions of human infinitesimality."[40] To summarize, weird monsters have no historical antecedent. They come from a radically nonhuman beyond, and as such, they suggest a worldview apposite the Anthropocene, a worldview that enjoins humanity to come to grips with its position in temporalities and spatialities beyond the scale at which thinking is comfortable or perhaps even possible.

While the recognition of humanity's infinitesimality remains necessary, it nonetheless suggests a residual critical attitude characteristic of the modern modes of knowledge that the Anthropocene undermines, which states that politics and history, in every one of their manifestations, are lies in need of debunking. Such an attitude leaves little room for rethinking politics and history outside of what Bruno Latour calls the critical stance[41]—an outside where fact becomes subordinated to concern. Lovecraft's narrators are often academic scientists whose capacities for madness are exploited by their discoveries of the Great Old Ones or the shoggoths, and which depend precisely on the scientists' certainty that the disciplinary frameworks through which they understand the world are up to the challenge of understanding it. They do not go mad from learning how this or that fact is wrong. Rather, they go mad because they learn how their assumptions—which allow them to understand things in terms of facts, which proceed from conditions that allow them to formulate meaningful narratives from such facts—have always already been wrong. Moreover, this wrongness is deep, and it is not subject to amelioration by way of further discovery. The ordering of any such discovery—the narrativization of any new fact—would itself rely on a humanist assumption about how facts can and should be ordered that would also turn out to be wrong in the face of weird ontology.

As Benjamin Noys and Timothy S. Murphy argue, "In contradiction to Lovecraft's horror at the alien, influenced by his racism, the new weird adopts a more radical politics that treats the alien, the hybrid, and the chaotic as subversions of the various normalizations of power."[42] We may sometimes find in the new weird monsters that exist beyond human comprehension—for example, Miéville's slake moths and Weavers in *Perdido Street Station*, Swainston's insects in *The Year of Our War*, and Felix Gilman's Line and Gun in *The Half-Made World* (2010). However, more often than not, these monsters solicit human sympathy and fascination even as they remain monstrous: Miéville's Re-made, grindylow, and anophelii; VanderMeer's flesh dogs, gray caps, Crawler, and Borne; the various monsters in Barker's short fiction. Consider these lines from Barker's short story "In the Hills, the Cities," in which two travelers encounter fighting monsters comprising the bodies of the denizens of two remote towns in communist-controlled Eastern Europe:

> The Englishmen remained where they stood, watching the spectacle as it approached. Neither dread nor horror touched them now, just an awe that rooted them to the spot. They knew this was a sight they could never hope to see again; this was the apex—after this there was only common experience. Better to stare then, though every step brought death nearer, better to stay and see the sight while it was there to be seen. And if it killed them, this monster, then at least they would have glimpsed a miracle, known this terrible majesty for a brief moment. It seemed a fair exchange.[43]

VanderMeer describes a similar, and long-standing, attraction to monstrosity in the introduction to his 2011 nonfiction collection, *Monstrous Creatures*: "From an early age, I think I had an appreciation for a definition of 'monstrous' that did not mean 'hideous,' 'horrible,' or 'ghastly … for me, the monstrous is the intersection of the beautiful with the strange, the dangerous with the sublime.'"[44] One can find similar sentiments, and similar moments of wonder or ecstasy, in the weird to be sure.[45] None of the distinctions between the weird and the new weird is perfect, except perhaps the periodization, and even that is complicated. However, the new weird exhibits a general tendency to espouse a world-view more open to and receptive of the beyond than does the weird. This worldview is embodied in the relationship between its monsters and those who encounter them.

As a final means by which to distinguish the weird from the new weird, and thereby contextualize VanderMeer's work generically, we can consider their respective deployments of primary and secondary worlds. Whereas the weird tends to set its stories in the primary world (i.e., the reader's world, what we might call the real world), the new weird often makes use of secondary worlds with often indiscernible relationships to the real world. Secondary worlds, the most famous of which is proba-bly J. R. R. Tolkien's Middle-earth, exist wholly apart from our own. In short, you can't get there from here by traveling through space or time.[46] Many weird fictions make use of ancient or far-future versions of earth. William Hope Hodgson's Night Land, Clark Ashton Smith's Zothique, and Robert Howard's Hyborian Age all exist in a relationship with the primary world that we might call geohistorical. Fictions by Lovecraft, Blackwood, and James take place in settings to which the reader might travel in space, even if these settings serve to eventually estrange. Although these worlds seem to have vastly different laws than those we understand to govern our daily lives, they nonetheless espouse some-thing like the weird worldview, one in which our comforting fictions, based on a necessarily limited understanding of our materiality, turn out to be merely that—fictions—by way of a radical and final act of critique.

In contrast, many of the best known new weird fictions are set in worlds whose ontologies are always already different than our own and therefore produce modes of thought altogether different than those that manifest in the primary world. Such secondary worlds include Miéville's Bas-Lag, Swainston's Fourlands, VanderMeer's Ambergris and its environs, the bleak landscape surrounding Bishop's Etched City, Paul di Filippo's Linear City, and Simon Ings's City of the Iron Fish.[47] If science fiction transformed and complicated the utopia by rendering difference in terms of time rather than space, then the new weird seems to transform the utopia, the place set apart from us spatially or historically, yet again by rendering the difference between here and there not in terms of time or space but rather by way of some other threshold we can but dimly discern, much less cross at will. VanderMeer's fiction manifests and exemplifies such thresholds.

Like the Anthropocene, which draws together nature and culture and which demonstrates the necessity of thinking both in relation to one another, the new weird deploys and inhabits hybridity, involution, attachment, assemblage, gathering, and entanglement. Likewise, the new weird is comparable to cultural geology, to which I turn next, in its new materialist form, which begins from the assumption of such togetherness in order to understand materiality in a more complex and fundamental sense than modern modes of thought have been able to articulate. The weird posited a beyond to which humans could have no relation, inhabited by monsters no human could sympathize with, in the name of the single fact that humanity means nothing. This worldview perhaps derives from the aftermath of World War I, when enduring national boundaries and identities were erased, and the Westphalian state, as well as the history within which it acted, was revealed as the fiction it always had been. Timothy S. Murphy claims that the weird can be understood as a geoliterature, "a model in which relations are prior to their terms—in other words, a model in which peoples, nation states, and their proprietary literatures are transitory surface effects rather than deep and eternal causal structures."[48] In contrast, the new weird manifests in a world in which national borders are always already permeable, even if this is far more the case for globalized capital than for individual actors. More importantly, the new weird manifests worlds whose modes of existence enjoy strange relationships with our own. It is a literature that understands its context and fights it on its own terms. It comprises a network of entities in temporary, fluid, emergent relations in combat against more of the same. It recognizes that the criticality of science fiction no longer works and that horror is only response to this situation. It deploys fantasy and its wonder, but it does so tempered by the fact that it can only put things back together, with the awareness that all such healing leaves scars.

CULTURAL GEOLOGY

As should be clear, the Anthropocene and new weird fiction do not, in this argument, represent new objects to know, but rather challenge what we call knowing. Since at least the beginning of the twenty-first century, scholars and thinkers have endeavored to meet this challenge by focusing on such objects as the Anthropocene and by developing modes of thought adequate to it. Mark McGurl describes scholarly attention to the Anthropocene as one of many "initiatives" that make up a new cultural geology: "A range of theoretical and other initiatives that position culture in a time-frame large enough to crack open the carapace of human self-concern, exposing it to the idea, and maybe even the fact, of its external ontological preconditions, its ground."[49] McGurl does not mean to suggest that the geologic epoch identified and defined by the term "Anthropocene" has no reality unto itself. Rather, he means that in addition to the epoch, the term has come to designate an approach to the conditions of human thought that takes as a starting assumption the fundamental interaction of subject and object, of the human individual or group and the material support on which the individual or group stands, and makes possible every action and thought for that individual or group even as it is transformed by such action and thought. I am here concerned with the latter sense of Anthropocene as a context in which, and a concept by which, we can understand how VanderMeer's fiction develops fantastic materialities, grounds on which we have never stood, conditions we have never inhabited.

McGurl draws together a number of philosophical and theoretical schools under the umbrella of cultural geology, including speculative realism, object-oriented ontology, and assemblage theory. To this list I would add actor–network theory and new materialism. I would also note that there is considerable overlap among these frameworks and considerable debates about the precise dimensions of each, as well as the utility of the terms that name them. Among the thinkers who fall into one or more of these categories, some of whom McGurl identifies and others I add here, are Karen Barad, Jane Bennett, Ray Brassier, Manuel De Landa, Elizabeth Grosz, Graham Harman, Bruno Latour, Quentin Meillassoux, Timothy Morton, Jussi Parikka, Elizabeth Povinelli, and Alexander Weheliye. Even where they oppose one another on major and minor issues, all of these groupings and individuals share a commitment to rethinking the human, especially in terms of its relationship to its interlocutors: the object, the environment, the earth, the ground, nature, media, materiality, reality. Some of these groupings, such as speculative realism and object-oriented ontology, claim in various ways that human thought has little or no access to the real objects it contemplates. Others, such as new materialism, seek to understand the interactions and relations among various entities under the assumption that these interactions and relations are thought. This is a thought that does not take place in a discrete mind according to the autonomous choice of an individual but rather as the emergent property of a complex assemblage, network, gathering, or entanglement. Insofar as these approaches all challenge the manner in which the human and its history have been separated from nature and its givenness, they all prove valuable in the present context. Each possesses a particular capacity to highlight various aspects of the material and intellectual conditions under which VanderMeer has produced his fiction. In the interests again of brevity and clarity, and in service to my larger arguments, I focus here on those initiatives that most clearly begin from the idea that materiality interacts with and shapes subjectivity and the manner in which that subjectivity shapes materiality in turn, namely those that fall broadly into what has been called new materialism, as well Bruno Latour's challenge to the critical stance of modern knowledge practices.

New materialism distinguishes itself from the historical materialism described by Marx and Marxists since the second half of the nineteenth century. Two passages from Marx will suffice to establish the nature of historical materialism, despite the complexity of the idea and the voluminous scholarship on the matter. Marx famously begins *The Eighteenth*

Brumaire of Louis Napoleon (1852) with the following claim: "Men make their own history, but not spontaneously, under conditions they have chosen for themselves; rather on terms immediately existing, given and handed down to them. The tradition of countless dead generations is an incubus to the mind of the living."[50] In other words, human thought and action does not take place in a vacuum or under neutral circumstances. It necessarily confronts, adopts, and engages with history, the thoughts and actions of the past insofar as they have produced the present as a precondition of the future. Later, in the postface to the second edition of *Capital*, Marx makes clear how his materialist dialectic must be distinguished from Hegel's idealist one:

> My dialectical method is, in its foundations, not only different
> from the Hegelian, but exactly opposite to it. For Hegel,
> the process of thinking, which he even transforms into an
> independent subject, under the name of 'the Idea,' is the
> creator of the real world, and the real world is only the external
> appearance of the idea. With me the reverse is true: the ideal is
> nothing but the material world reflected in the mind of man,
> and translated into forms of thought.[51]

For Francis Fukuyama, Hegelian history, in which communism and capitalism confront one another as ideal forms of human organization, came to an end in the late 1980s with the triumph of one ideal over the other (even if material reality did not keep pace with this triumph). As opposed to Hegel, Marx does indeed offer a materialist account of history. However, insofar as nature only ever seems to appear in Marx's history by way of human labor and the value it grants to nature by way of its efforts, this historical materialism remains a process in which human meaning maintains only a limited and roundabout relation to the material world which conditions it.[52]

New materialism questions the assumption that nature only means something to the human insofar as the human produces from its raw materials objects with value for humans, and insofar as the human draws nature into its own sphere of influence.[53] In terms of my argument, new materialism on the one hand challenges claims that nature ends because the human historicizes it through its interventions. On the other hand, it also challenges claims that history operates independently of, or is even constitutive of, the natural world. For example, in *A Thousand Years of Nonlinear History*, Manuel De Landa, drawing on Gilles Deleuze and Félix Guattari's concept of the machinic phylum and Fernand Braudel's investigations of history and geography, demonstrates how the present has not been determined simply by human endeavor; nor is it the outcome of a closed system approaching equilibrium, the latter of which underpins Fukuyama's claim that history can end. De Landa admits that historians must account for human beliefs and desires in any description of the past because such "expectations and preferences are what guide human decision making in a wide range of social activities, such as politics and economics."[54] These beliefs and desires may be constrained or channeled by other beliefs and desires, whether of individuals or of institutions and groups.

However, history does not begin or end with such anthropocentric concerns. "In other cases," writes De Landa, "what matters is not the planned results of decision making, but the *unintended collective consequences* of human decisions."[55] The Anthropocene, as Chakrabarty argues, is such an unintended consequence of the human species and remains largely invisible to traditional notions of history as such. However, new materialist accounts of the world do not stop with this acknowledgment, which remains of a piece with Marx's claims about historical materialism. It proceeds to demonstrate the interaction of such collective decision making with the natural world and the emergence of what we might understand as naturalized or ontologized history. As John Durham Peters puts it, "Ontology, whatever else it is, is usually just forgotten infrastructure."[56] Such an understanding of the interactions among human subjects and natural objects informs De Landa's demonstration of the impact interrelated materialities of stone, genes, and language have on the shape of human civilization. It informs Nicole Starosielski's investigations of how the legacy of colonialism and imperialism as well as the topography of the ocean floor determine the routes of the contemporary undersea cables responsible for carrying the majority of the world's Internet traffic.[57] It informs Jussi Parikka's discussion of how human meaning depends on the media that produce and transmit it, media which in turn are constructed from geologic resources mined from the earth as well as the economic and political inequalities that make such mining possible.[58] Perhaps most broadly, it informs Karen Barad, who argues, "Matter and meaning are not separate elements. They are inextricably fused together, and no event, no matter how energetic, can tear them asunder."[59]

Although VanderMeer's fantastic materialities are of his own invention, new materialism provides means by which we might grasp how these materialities operate and what they offer us for thinking in and about the Anthropocene. It does so in two respects. First, it makes visible the manner in which materiality, the ground the human subject stands on and assumes when it thinks, in part determines the meanings humans make and how those meanings reciprocally determine the nature of the ground. Second, new materialism refuses the logic of representation that underpins historical materialist accounts of literature and thereby opens up new forms of thought capable of grasping the meaning of the material literary object. This second point is especially important to my purpose here. VanderMeer's worlds refuse to be reductive or allegorical, insofar as they do not simply map our present concerns. They likewise refuse to be deductive or historical, insofar as they do not simply follow from our present condition in a traceable, derivative fashion.

To clarify this point in the present context, consider one famous historical materialist account of how materiality determines literary production. In *The Political Unconscious*, Fredric Jameson states that the conflicts endemic to the economic mode of production of a given society—for example, late capitalism—express themselves in the cultural productions of that society. However, this expression is always of a human narrative and the conflicts thereof. Jameson argues, following a citation of Marx and Engels's claim that the "history of all hitherto existing society is the history of class struggles," that his "doctrine of the political unconscious finds its function and necessity" in "detecting the traces of that uninterrupted narrative, in restoring to the surface of the text the repressed and buried reality of this fundamental history."[60] New materialism does not deny the existence of such narrative, the importance of class struggle in the process of historical transformation, or the possibility of the interpretation of such narrative according to Jameson's methods. However, it makes clear that literature does not only function as a representation or expression of something external to it, something that it makes meaningful by way of encoding it into a human-readable form and at a human readable scale, whether that something is another textual system or brute materiality. If it did not offer some other means of understanding the literary text, new materialism could do no more than render the materiality of VanderMeer's worlds intelligible. It would only be able to do so in terms of how that materiality does or does not accurately reflect some aspect of our own materiality or in terms of how it derives from our own materiality through an historical process.[61] However, by way of showing how the earth, media, atoms, and other material entities entangle themselves with humanity and enjoy reciprocal relations of production with the human (among other entities), new materialism suggests that literature possesses a materiality, and therefore a force, of its own.

The constant and implicit demand by historical materialists that literary texts represent, and thus work through, historical problems is part and parcel of the critical stance that Bruno Latour rethinks in a 2004 essay.[62] Following earlier work, Latour argues that the demonstration that facts, which appeal directly to the "real world," are constructed should not be a cause of consternation among scholars and other interested parties who wish to ground their claims in truth in the face of right wing political opposition to what has been called "the reality-based community," "people who 'believe that solutions emerge from your judicious study of discernible reality.'"[63] For Latour, matters of fact only cohere by way of concern, by way of gathering together various bits of matter and discourse as things, things that come to mean something to those who participate in the gathering together. He writes:

> Whatever the words [that designate these gatherings], what is presented here is an entirely different attitude than the critical one, not a flight into the conditions of possibility of a given

matter of fact, not the addition of something more human that the inhumane matter of fact would have missed, but, rather, a multifarious inquiry launched with the tools of anthropology, philosophy, metaphysics, history, sociology, to detect *how many participants* are gathered in a *thing* to make it exist and to maintain its existence.[64]

These participants are not only subjects in the conventional sense but also are the many objects of the world now endowed with partial subjectivities that interact with the partial objectivities revealed in the now-displaced modern individual.

For Latour, objects may partake of any number of modes of existence, each of which possesses its own capacities to affect the world and be affected by it, to materially gather with or attach to its others. Latour, as summarized by Yves Citton, tells us that the critic, instead of merely interpreting texts or even "acting upon" them in order to take them to task, must "reorient the interpretive performance of the texts toward a more explicitly constructive use of its affordance. Instead of asking what our interpretation can *undo* (totalitarianism, capitalism, colonialism, sexism, mastery, fundamentalism, etc.), we are invited to ask what it can *make* (a platform of negotiation? a mapping of controversies? a lexicon of sanity?)."[65] Fictions in this understanding are but one entity on a flattened ontological plane, not (only) representations of reality that must be unpacked by readers who possess some interpretive master code that reveals them to be critical of the economic mode of production or symptomatic of it but also participants in reality by way of their particular mode of existence. This mode of existence, the being of fiction Latour refers to as "[FIC]," interacts with entities possessing the same or another mode of existence. Latour notes that [FIC] "does not direct our attention toward illusion, toward falsity, but toward what is fabricated, consistent, real." He further notes that the adverb "'fictitiously' immediately engages *all that follows* in a certain form of reality that cannot be confused with any other," even if a modern sensibility would deprive this certain form of reality of its ontological weight by determining it as merely symbolic of something else with a greater claim to the real.[66]

For Citton, the consequences of [FIC]'s ontological status are profound, yet obvious: "A human-centered plot, which never and nowhere 'existed' in the first place . . . , does indeed have a certain mode of 'existence,' since it does affect us, sometimes quite profoundly. We (really) care about fictional characters . . . . Our encounter with them often alters and shapes our worldview, our perceptions, our attention, our behaviors—sometimes more significantly than do our encounters with 'real' human beings."[67] In the present context, Latour makes possible a reading of VanderMeer's fictions as ontological entities in their own right. They possess the capacity to represent the entanglements of subjects and objects, of individuals and the grounds on which they stand and think. They also intervene into such entanglements by way of their participation in them. Latour thus allows us to engage with all materiality by way of a cultural geology that renders visible the manner in which cultural production is always materially of the earth even when it is not symbolically about it.

FANTASTIC MATERIALITY

Fantastic materiality implies a realistic or perhaps mimetic one—a normal materiality of this world against which it can be distinguished. The abnormality of the situation with which *Finch* opens demonstrates the possibility of normal in Ambergris, whatever form it takes and however absent it has become. In turn, the fantastic materiality in *Finch* might seem to reveal our own world's true materiality by providing us with much needed difference against which to measure the sameness of our own lives. Although we can indeed productively read *Finch* in this manner, this is not simply the case. As Gerry Canavan and Andrew Hageman claim, if there was ever a normal, there is none now. We live in "postnormal" times,[68] both naturally by way of the Anthropocene and historically by way of the election of Donald J. Trump to the American presidency and the reemergence of nationalism, white supremacy, and other right-wing movements into mainstream public discourse. Global systems have become weird to the extent that we understand their entanglements, attachments, and involutions at all. No materiality, fantastic or otherwise, will reveal a true and neutral standard, a norm against which this weirdness can be judged. Thus my argument here is not in the service of a return to some Edenic, pristine, unfallen past when things were not weird; nor does it point to an arrival in some utopian future when they will not be weird once again. Rather, it demonstrates how texts such as *Finch* negotiate weirdness by participating in it.

But what, then, is fantastic materiality? *None of This Is Normal* is the answer to this question, but first I offer some preliminary remarks.

As I have suggested, insofar as fantastic materiality can be connected to new materialism, it stands in opposition to certain tenets of historical materialism. Beyond that argument, I deploy the term "fantastic materiality" as an inversion of another term with strong ties to historical materialism and its methods, "science fiction." In a definition that still has resonance within the scholarship on the subject, as a starting point for dissent if nothing else, Darko Suvin notes that science fiction involves on one hand a world *"radically or at least significantly different from the empirical times, places, and characters* of 'mimetic' or 'naturalist' fiction,"* and, on the other hand situations "perceived as *not impossible* within the cognitive (cosmological and anthropological) norms of the author's epoch."[69] Thus Suvin outlines his claim that science fiction is the literature of cognitive estrangement, the literature that represents difference produced by historical means according to norms, necessities, or possibilities endemic to the primary world in which the writer writes and in which the reader reads. Carl Freedman draws on and transform Suvin's work in order to demonstrate the degree to which science fiction is a fundamentally critical genre, one committed at its best to history and its materiality.[70] However, in a postnormal or weird world, genre criticism cannot afford to continue to assume the materiality that grounds its thought. For Suvin, "science fiction" may be synonymous with "cognitive estrangement," but in the present context, it seems to be equally synonymous with "reality representation." In other words, science fiction seems to designate a given world encoded in a symbolic structure. Readers thus lose this world's materiality in their critical attempts to decode the symptomological by-products of the original encoding. The world's capacity to be accurately encoded, actually or potentially, is often questioned, but not in such a way that produces new forms of fiction or thought.

I do not mean to suggest that science fiction is ever only such an encoding, but rather that critics too often approach it as such—along with nearly every other form of cultural production. Nonetheless, the extent to which science fiction has never been able to represent the future it desires, according to the condition called history, reveals the extent to which it is limited by its involvement with modern and historical forms of thought. As Fredric Jameson argued decades ago, the utopia has long been about the impossibility of achieving utopia rather than actually producing it or representing it.[71] William Gibson's Blue Ant trilogy[72] and *The Peripheral* (2014); Richard Morgan's *Market Forces* (2004); Simon Ings's *Wolves* (2014); and other recent "presentist" science fictions suggests that the problem of imagining a future that does not derive simply (or even complexly) from present conditions in an historical fashion is not likely to go away anytime soon. Similarly, recent space operas (such as James S. A. Correy's The Expanse, 2001–, or Iain M. Banks's Culture novels, 1987–2012) seem almost quaint insofar as they present technological and material conditions that in no way conform to present understandings of science, and therefore appear to be fantasies of escape from the actual material conditions that produce them. Other space operas, such as Kim Stanley Robinson's *Aurora* (2015), devote themselves to demonstrating the impossibility of one of science fiction's paradigmatic conventions—the generation starship—actually saving us from the material conditions we have helped to create for ourselves. In the wake of science fiction's failure, we have seen the rise of the new weird as well as other new forms of fantasy (by, for example, Nnedi Okorafor and N. K. Jemisin) dedicated to reimagining the boundaries of the possible by way of ignoring the constraints that history and science determine for those boundaries.

Fantastic materiality does not solve the problem I have just described, but it does not seek to. The problem with this problem has to do with both the way it is formulated and the answers that formulation demands and affords. For critical thought, based as it is on a materiality becoming fantastic before our very eyes—or, better, becoming fantastic apparently quickly after having done so slowly—history is a problem to solve that can only be solved by way of more history. I acknowledge the degree to which this recursive structure constrains our thought generally and my thought specifically, but I seek to describe something else—something that does not merely refer back to or derive from this structure even if it was produced under the condition of this structure. Thus fantastic materiality inverts science fiction. "Fantastic," of course, refers to a story, a production, a construction, an imagining, a creation—in short, a fiction. The fantastic is not real. Nonetheless, because it has no truck with preconceptions of what reality is, it undoes the critical opposition between a reality that is given and the representations we make of it. Its materiality, which replaces science and its disciplinary assumptions in my inversion, has to do with the conditions it creates and represents within its stories. Much more importantly, it has to do with the materiality with which it entangles itself and thereby transforms by way of the effects its fantasies have on and for readers. In short, the significance of this inversion might be summarized as follows. Fantastic tracks with fiction and materiality with science, but I do not posit a materialist fantasy or a materialist fantastic. In the formulation of science fiction, the world and its allegedly immutable, discoverable truth provides a measuring stick for the quality of the story told about it. In contrast, in fantastic materiality, the narrative itself (the fantastic) modifies the world (materiality) in order to overcome such critical practices and thereby introduce to a world without predetermined notions of reality the means by which to change it. Fantastic materiality does not tell stories that are true in some way, according to a given materiality or empirical world out there against which they can be judged. It is a materiality that transforms by way of fantasies entangled with that world.

2

LET ME TELL YOU ABOUT THE CITY

THE VENISS MILIEU AND THE PROBLEM OF SETTING

VENISS: TEXTS, NARRATIVE, MILIEU

Veniss, or rather the Veniss milieu, is Jeff VanderMeer's first significant creation.[1] From the point of view of the twenty-first century, the Veniss milieu might appear to be a conventional science fictional, dystopian, or apocalyptic setting, in which biotechnological progress and catastrophic climate change continue their inevitable developments and thus combine to produce a world lethal to humanity in a manner readers can understand as originating in the material conditions of their own world. Although the Veniss texts—whether taken individually or collectively organized into an overall narrative of ongoing, manifold collapse—invite such a reading, it would miss how the milieu resists setting and the critical and historicist assumptions on which setting depends. A careful analysis of the milieu will account for the heterogeneous nature of the texts describing it, readers' capacities to order these texts, and the

nonhuman and other material agencies at work in the milieu. This analysis will thus begin to outline what a fantastic materiality looks like: one
that denies any apparent convention.

In their development of a milieu (the term literally means "middle
place"), the Veniss texts and the overall (if discontinuous) story they
relate suggest that solving problems of scale and representation characteristic of the Anthropocene requires undoing or reconfiguring the
delimited times and spaces of setting, which serves as a vehicle for or
container of meaning. In general, neither longer narratives that afford
greater description nor narratives that take place over extended periods of time or in larger spaces (terrestrial, galactic, or even cosmic) will
overcome the shortcomings of setting as a delimitation of narrative
space and time in this regard. Such narratives would still rely on explicit
or implicit end points: those provided by the limits of the printed page
or the bound book, or those constructed by way of carving a delimited
and therefore graspable here and now from an incomprehensible everywhere and always. Such texts would merely provide bigger containers for
meaning—containers that would therefore maintain the anthropomorphic and anthropocentric assumptions behind meaning itself.

In Amitav Ghosh's specific argument, and in general discussions
of modern literature, setting, which "allows most stories to unfold,"
depends on discontinuities that isolate particular times and spaces from
other times and spaces.[2] These discontinuities enjoin the wider world,
in which settings manifest as self-contained globes, to recede from view
and from knowledge (even if this wider world continues to condition
setting). They thus produce a limited space and time, an anthropomorphic and anthropocentric space and time. This space and this time,
taken together, are the condition of human-scaled meaning, which is
to say meaning tout court. The operations that produce setting are certainly capable of questioning themselves in a properly critical manner,
and they often do, although without questioning their ultimate ground,
turning inward and away from materiality and therefore from the planetary scale and conditions the Anthropocene involves. Likewise, they
produce more truthful accounts of the world by way of this ignorance,
but these truths are measured in terms of the limited spaces and times in

which they take place. This chapter makes use of Ghosh's understanding of setting in relation to the problem of representing the Anthropocene as a point of contrast for a discussion of Veniss as a milieu; it does so to more generally demonstrate how the limitations imposed by setting exclude an understanding of nonhuman space and time beyond an anthropocentric or anthropomorphic one. The Veniss milieu remains, of course, a human construction, and therefore, like a conventional setting, it exists within limits (the pages on which accounts of it are printed, if nothing else). Likewise, careful readers may be able to glean from the texts that describe the milieu a geographical and/or temporal relationship to their own world, albeit one that will always remain questionable and obscure. It nonetheless challenges the conventional, novelistic notion of setting and points the way toward a weird space and time in which a transformed humanity might exist, one that does not force a choice among the pure belonging found in fantasy, the cognitive estrangement found in science fiction, and the pure estrangement found in horror.

Before I turn my attention to theoretical matters and attendant discussions of how specific Veniss texts address and overcome the limitations of setting, a brief description of the texts and the Veniss narrative will help to clarify the nature of the milieu. This nature is not set but remains always weirdly dynamic.[3] VanderMeer describes the Veniss milieu over the course of ten published texts, none of which work in quite the same manner or seem to refer to quite the same set of spatial and temporal coordinates. In fact, as a term, "the Veniss milieu," which I adopt from VanderMeer's own designation of the city and its surroundings, is misleading in one respect. Namely, the city called Veniss, theoretically positioned and locatable in some here and now, only appears in some of the following texts, and in many cases it only exists for the reader as something recalled from other texts. This lack of reference to Veniss, however, only serves to make my point that the milieu refuses setting and the assumptions thereof. In any case, the Veniss cycle roughly takes the following internal chronology: "The Sea, Mendeho, and Moonlight" (short story, 1990); "Veniss Exposed" (short story, 2003); "Flesh" (short story, 1991); *Veniss Underground* (novel, 2003); "Detectives and Cadavers" (short story, 1992); "Jessible and the Metal Dragon" (fragment, 2006); "A Heart for Lucretia" (short story, 1993); "Balzac's War" (novella, 1997); "The City" (short story, 2004); and "Three Days in a Border Town" (short story, 2004).[4]

Aside from the experiences of the various characters who populate them, taken together these texts describe what seems to be a city or region located on a far-future and increasingly uninhabitable earth, but in isolation from the earth generally. (In "Detectives and Cadavers," the situation is described thusly: "Getting out of Veniss had been problematic, demonstrators surrounding the front portal as ever: doomsayers convinced that the city's growing isolation from other Earth enclaves was directly related to the muttie expulsion and supposed 'persecution' of the Funny People.")[5] However, despite the ordering I provide here, these texts and the individual narratives they contain refuse to finally cohere into a clear overall history or exhibit a consistent, identifiable form of causality that would allow readers to connect them with one another; they refuse to exclude nonanthropomorphic and nonanthropocentric aspects of materiality. In doing so they become unwilling and incapable of saying that *this* leads to *that* in some straightforward manner necessarily relevant to human being or knowledge, of claiming that this (human) moment or place is significant by way of the exclusion of a distinct (nonhuman) time or place. Because they achieve this result mainly as a consequence of their complex textuality, suggested by this brief account, they require that readers interact with them and come to terms not only with the human agencies that inhabit them but also with the nonhuman material forces hinted at but never fully seen within their pages. Thus readers' recollections and coordinations of these texts serve less to create a larger or more coherent story for Veniss than they force readers to exist in the middle of the texts themselves and never situate themselves at a specific point—that is, in a setting.

Any description of the overall Veniss narrative will obscure the forces it involves precisely because such narrativization works to the degree that it undertakes such obfuscation. Nonetheless, a brief account of the overall Veniss narrative is necessary to the discussion that follows. As the narrative begins, humanity (or that part of it which inhabits the milieu—the difference between set and subset is unclear) lives under the stultifying managerial schemes of artificial intelligences called soliminds. At some imprecise date, a civil war among these machines leaves Veniss without any proper or obvious governmental, economic, or social structure. The earliest of the Veniss texts, in terms of both chronology and publication date, is "The Sea, Mendeho, and Moonlight." It describes the situation before this civil war and tells the story of an old man, Mendeho, who defies the soliminds by swimming out to sea, as he had done in his youth (when Veniss was known as Dayton Central). His death by drowning ultimately becomes a myth with many versions, with one for spacefarers, another for the landlocked, and so on. This myth serves to reinforce the soliminds' power, at least for a time: "Yes, the solimind has decided, myths can be useful things. For in all the tales the old man Mendeho drifts out to sea, space, or pasture on a destiny of the solimind's making and is never seen again."[6]

As the rule of the soliminds collapses, a boy named Bunadeo—"created, nurtured, and birthed in a vat"—grows up to be the Living Artist and "bioneer" Quin.[7] As Quin, Bunadeo gains considerable power in Veniss, even if the means by which he wields this power remain inscrutable. Quin expands on the work of his creator and mentor, perfecting an intelligent species of meerkat with opposable thumbs. *Veniss Underground* begins with a young man named Nicholas, who, with his twin sister Nicola, was likely created by Quin for no discernible reason. Nicholas desires an audience with Quin in order to procure a meerkat, claiming that this will save him from living out the rest of his life in a "garbage zone." The precise reasons why he believes that such an acquisition, and the relationship it might help Nicholas forge with Quin, might save him remain unclear. In his quest, Nicholas ignores the advice of Shadrach, one of Quin's employees and Nicola's former lover, about how to deal with Quin. After he disappears on his quest, Nicola searches for him and is eventually taken captive by Quin. Quin, who believes he may dispose of his creations as he desires, begins to sell off Nicola's body parts (an eye, a hand) to rich patrons and causes Shadrach to become aware of his cruelty. Shadrach, in an act that mirrors the journey of Orpheus into the underworld to find Eurydice, goes in search of Nicola. After a series of adventures and encounters reminiscent of Dante's experience in hell,

Shadrach confronts Quin, who explains, first, that he has passed beyond all notions of the human, and second, that he has put into motion events that will lead to the end of humanity more broadly. Specifically, his biotechnological creations are in the process of revolting against "natural" humans in defense of the "natural" world (from which, like humans, they have been alienated). Shadrach kills Quin, perhaps accelerating this revolution, and escapes with Nicola. Like Orpheus, Shadrach looks back as he and Nicola make their escape. Unlike Eurydice, Nicola finds her way out of the darkness nonetheless. However, this victory remains radically localized, never again referenced by the Veniss texts and without any apparent consequence for the overall Veniss milieu.

In a story that takes place during or immediately after *Veniss Underground*, "Detectives and Cadavers," a detective discovers a dead beast. As he witnesses its resurrection, he states, in a passage whose specific reference is clear and general significance enigmatic, "The flesh is reforming. Coming back to life."[8] Subsequent Veniss texts suggest, although never make clear, that this specific beast belongs to a more general revolution of the flesh that comprises Quin's meerkats as well as so-called mutties and Funny People. In the present story, the beast and its immediate allies attack "natural" or "normal" humanity. This attack begins the process of driving humanity out of Veniss and Bathalkazar, Veniss's sister city, although this process remains largely unnarrated. By the time of "Jessible and the Metal Dragon" and "A Heart for Lucretia," humans have fled into the desert wasteland Shadrach once traveled through on missions for Quin—a wasteland most of humanity had avoided as fundamentally dangerous. In this new environment, the threat of biotechnologically created beasts and the reality of catastrophic climate change have apparently destroyed traditional familial, social, and political structures. Humans have reorganized themselves into crèches for the purposes of raising their young and mere subsistence. These crèches survive in the desert, which may or may not still be near the sea in which Mendeho swam and drowned. (Geography, never certain to begin with, becomes less and less clear as the overall narrative accrues.)

They do so until a boy named Gerard, in "A Heart for Lucretia," undertakes a quest to find a human heart for his twin sister, who has a genetic cardiovascular disease. He travels to a ruined Veniss (although he does not know the city by that, or any, name). There he encounters the meerkats, who have taken over the underground world in which they once served Quin. (Quin has been entirely erased from human, and perhaps meerkat, memory by this point.[9]) The meerkats take Gerard and his companion, Flesh Dog, below level, and in exchange for one of their last human hearts, conduct experiments on them. In "Balzac's War," the results of this experiment, flesh dogs joined to human heads that retain the power to speak but remain unaware of their hybrid condition, attack and terrorize another pocket of humanity that had inadvertently drawn attention to itself while exploring the ruins of Balthakazar. Although the outcome of this war remains unclear, the dire straits humanity finds itself in at the end of the novella suggest there can be no survival, much less triumph, for this obsolete species.

In "The City," the penultimate Veniss text, manta ray–like familiars symbiotically or parasitically attach themselves to the remnants of humanity who search for an obscure, miragelike city in an endless desert. The familiars feed memories to individual humans, which these humans only dimly understand. It remains unclear whether there is any city any more, or, for that matter, any place where humans might survive. It also remains unclear whether there are any humans. Further complicating this story is the fact that "The City" does not reveal itself to be a clear part of the Veniss milieu by way of any internal reference or mechanism. VanderMeer suggests in a note appended to the version of "The City" published in *Secret Life* that there may be such a relationship, but only in "Three Days in a Border Town" does this relationship become concrete by internal reference (albeit a fleeting one that serves to underscore the overall obscurity of the milieu). In this final Veniss text, a woman only identified as "you" searches for her lost husband, who may or may not have been welcomed into the city that has long eluded the people who populate "The City." As she searches the border towns that "surround" and "mirror" the city (how can something surround or mirror a free-floating mirage?), she writes and compiles *The Book of the City*, a text whose truth remains always questionable insofar as its referent remains forever unknowable, but nonetheless seems to be gospel for the woman who constructs it.

In the end, she makes contact with a familiar that may be able to help her in her quest, but whether she will succeed remains unclear.

Numerous inconsistencies complicate the narrative I have here offered, as well as the causality it implies. In some cases these inconsistencies may be explained as the consequences of world building across multiple, disparate texts.[10] Such inconsistencies accrue again and again, for example in comic universes and in franchises, as their narratives develop, as their conflicts proliferate, and as their characters spread out in a setting.[11] However, the Veniss milieu exhibits deeper and more profound inconsistencies, ones that will remind readers of those found in the proto–new weird works of M. John Harrison, whose Pastel City in the *Viriconium* stories (1971–85) so dramatically changes from one tale to the next that readers can never be certain they are encountering the same place twice, or Mervyn Peake, whose Gormenghast Castle of the Gormenghast novels (1946–59) exists entirely apart not only from the world itself but from world as an organizing principle. In fact, the term "inconsistency" is here misleading, suggesting as it does a potential consistency that has, through act or omission, failed to emerge. What I have called inconsistencies are, properly understood, rather discontinuities, but discontinuities quite different from those characteristic of setting. They do not disappear by way of progress or the acquisition of further knowledge as they would, for example, by way of exploration or the study of geography. Quite to the contrary. These discontinuities refuse to assume a potential continuity that will manifest at some later date by one means or another. They run deeper than such knowledge practices can penetrate precisely because the milieu finally resists such ordering in a qualitative rather than quantitative fashion. That is, it resists ordering weirdly. These discontinuities are constitutive of the Veniss milieu and fundamental to understanding it as a milieu in contrast to setting. They are fundamental to its materiality.

As I suggest above, some of the Veniss texts do not take place in Veniss, and relatively few of them even mention the city by name. Even when they do reference the city itself, they continually disavow all claims to concrete knowledge about it, to the point where the designation "Veniss" can be nothing but the most conventional convention, a signifier without any anchor in conceptual or material reality beyond the insistence of those who use it. These texts refuse to ground or situate themselves in a well-bounded space and time—that is, a setting. This refusal is part and parcel of their capacity to overcome or circumvent the problem of scale. This problem will compromise the ability of any narrative that attempts to index geologic or cosmological forces to a human standard to adequately address the nonhuman world. As an example of how the Veniss texts disavow knowledge of the milieu, consider the opening line of the longest of these texts, *Veniss Underground*: "Let me tell you about the city."[12] This invitation to knowledge, repeated as the last line of part one of the novel, comes from Nicholas, a would-be but untalented Living Artist far more confident in his abilities than his life experience warrants. He does, however, offer the reader a few small bits of information about the city, Veniss: that its Social Revolutions (whatever they were or are) played a decisive role in the end of Old Art, and that it was once known as Dayton Central before taking on the nickname Veniss, "like an adder's hiss, deadly and unpredictable," after the collapse of its central government.[13] He does not, and likely cannot, tell the reader much more. However, as ignorant as he is, and though this ignorance will land him in a garbage zone, Nicholas's inability to say anything meaningful or useful about the city—how it operates now, where its borders are located, what lies beyond its walls, what its social norms are, how it compares with other cities, what the rest of earth now looks like—does not derive from some inherent lack fundamental to his character or being; nor does it involve a failure of formal or informal educational systems that suffice for others but not for him.

Shadrach, whose words of advice Nicholas fails to heed, provides a counterpoint to Nicholas's apparent ignorance or stupidity. Shadrach was born and raised in the underground below Veniss, surrounded by the garbage zones Nicholas fears. He works for Quin, the nominal ruler of the underground. In the course of his employment, he not only moves with relative freedom among Veniss's many autonomous districts, past the security checkpoints that divide populations from one another. He also travels outside the city's walls, into the desert wasteland between Veniss and Balthakazar. In theory Shadrach knows as much about the

Veniss milieu as anyone, and certainly more than nearly every other character we encounter in the novel, especially Nicholas, with the possible exception of Quin. Nonetheless, as he prepares to enter the underground, Shadrach struggles to understand it: "*Why* such a place should exist was a question hopelessly tangled in other questions, lost in the below level passageways, long ago."[14] He fails to comprehend the underground because in the Veniss milieu, questions have not only lost their answers but also lack something even more essential: their ability to distinguish themselves from other questions.

To take this point a step further, the Veniss milieu excludes the sort of critical and historicist questions that would lead to any explanation of what it is, questions that might in some fashion limit it or situate it at a scale amenable to human knowledge.[15] For historicist knowledge, every question can be answered (well or otherwise), and answered questions create the conditions for further questions that can in turn be answered. For critical knowledge, questions can themselves be questioned, and these metainterrogations produce better and better questions with regard to reality. However, each form of questioning assumes something it claims to produce: delimited times and spaces in which they themselves operate and that grant them meaning or guarantee their upstandingness. Veniss as a milieu rejects the end points such questioning provides and assumes.

I shall return to the milieu in the final section of this chapter, where I focus on two of the Veniss texts, "Balzac's War" and "The City," insofar as they describe the peculiar refugee status of the inhabitants of the milieu—a refugee status that involves fleeing from the conventional delimitations on time and space imposed by setting. For now, I turn my attention to matters of genre, setting, and representation in order to clarify how the milieu resists anthropomorphic and anthropocentric knowledge practices.

GENRE, SETTING, AND THE PROBLEM OF REPRESENTATION

The various subgenres of fantastika on which the new weird draws, and which it seeks to transform, can be distinguished from one another in part by way of their approach to setting.[16] Fantasy, for which the Fall is a fall precisely into history and the limitations history deploys in order to make meaning for the human, idealizes the Land. The Land, an Edenic paradise corrupted by the Fall, is not a setting insofar as it refuses the limitations of setting and thereby grants to subjects a perfect form of belonging that is not compromised by local or passing concerns. We might call this belonging magical. The conflict in fantasy thus involves overcoming limitation in an attempt to return to what Peter Sloterdjik might term the "perfect sphere" of death.[17] Tolkien's Lothlórien suggests such a realm, which can only exist for the human in the perfection of an unquestionable story—the sort often told to children.

Science fiction, by contrast, assumes setting even if it expands the temporal and spatial boundaries that characterize the settings of the mimetic novel. In its search for a utopia (or dystopia) beyond historical processes, science fiction imagines a leap out of or beyond the limitations setting imposes by way of final critical or historical operations that neither critique nor history can produce according to their own assumptions. Even the best science fiction assumes setting in this manner. Ursula K. Le Guin's *The Dispossessed* (1974) begins with a circle that either keeps an entire planet in or the rest of the universe out, thus delimiting both spaces. In Samuel R. Delany's *Stars in My Pocket Like Grains of Sand* (1984), the universe comprises thousands of internally heterogeneous planets, but even the implicit thousands upon thousands of cultures that these planets support nonetheless suggest a setting, although it is a complex one to be sure.

Finally, horror (especially in its weird mode) seeks to undermine the notion of setting by demonstrating the degree to which humans require times and spaces that are anthropocentric and anthropomorphic, in terms of their physical scale but also in terms of their conceptual friendliness, in order to make their way on a planet hostile to their meaningful existences. As such, the Veniss milieu most closely resembles the "settings" of horror in that it exposes human beings to situations that undo their relationships to isolated times and spaces, relationships mandated and required by their sense of being human. However, horror often leaves humans in this exposed state, as if to imply an unbreakable relationship between individuals and groups on the one hand, and the knowledge practices that render individuals and groups human on the other hand. When, for example, the narrator of Algernon Blackwood's *The Willows* (1907) confronts the elemental forces of the Danube, he finds himself unable to come to any understanding of what faces him; he fails to recognize understanding itself as the limitation to his becoming. Only a human sacrifice can appease these forces, with which there can be no common cause for the human. The scientists of H. P. Lovecraft's *At the Mountains of Madness* (1936) face a similar dilemma in that they can never communicate with the shoggoths, much less with the even more monstrous forces only hinted at in the conclusion to the novel. While the Veniss milieu remains in many respects close to this form of horror, it nonetheless offers an early example of the sorts of worlds VanderMeer develops—worlds in which a weird or ecstatic relationship of the human to the nonhuman remains not only possible but also necessary, even desirable. These worlds may finally destroy humanity, but such destruction is merely another form of transformation.

Although my sketch of these genres only describes within them general tendencies that may be refuted by individual texts and subgenres, it nonetheless suggests how previous types of fiction—even those committed to inhuman, posthuman, or transhuman modes of being—maintain a convention, setting, that limits knowledge to a certain humanist scale and form. This limitation only becomes clearer when read against the new weird, which identifies and draws out the countertendencies within these genres by way of its hybridizing project.[18] The new weird is not, of course, alone in this project of erasing the boundaries humans create for the purpose of containing meaning and thereby coming to grips with the materiality that these boundaries force to recede. It remains one shared by the various projects Mark McGurl groups under the heading cultural geology. As I discussed in chapter 1, such theoretical considerations of the Anthropocene reveal how modern human categories and concepts such as history and nature, insofar as they seek to isolate various phenomena, events, or conditions from one another and thereby make them accessible to human knowledge, fail to grasp the scales at which the Anthropocene operates. We might acknowledge the massive timescales at which climate change and geologic transformation take place, but we cannot perceive them from the points of view afforded by either our limited life spans or the isolated bits of ground on which we stand. Certainly our narrative forms, indexed as they so often are to such life spans and the peripeteias thereof, generally fail to make these timescales accessible to readers. Even those individual narratives that span the earth, moving from one continent and nation to the next geographically, can never capture the earth qua the materiality of geologic events. Such is the case because our narrative forms, such as the novel, move along abstract and abstracting axes. They travel along lines of latitude and longitude when they take us from one place to another and thereby demonstrate the differences among various locations. They traverse altitudes, taking readers above the earth or below the sea. They move us forward and backward through time by way of any number of tropes and conventions, and thereby relate the various instances they represent to one another implicitly or explicitly in terms of both similarity and difference.

However, in every case, these narrative forms remain limited by human knowledge practices. They may set themselves in many places concurrently or consecutively, but they never involve everywhere at once (even if everywhere remains limited to this planet, or even just its surface). When they involve places in the air, below the sea, or even below the earth, they do so by mobilizing anthropocentric boxes isolated from the inhuman environment—airplane or ship cabins, for example—to serve as containers of human life and meaning.[19] As they move through time, these narrative forms necessarily eliminate time. No narrative can account for all the time it encompasses, every moment of every day to which it refers. Experimental writing that attempts to capture the totality of a limited time from a limited point of view—such as Harry Mathews's *The Journalist* (1994) or Kenneth Goldsmith's *Fidget* (1997)—inevitably winds up being about its failures rather than its successes, much in the way that utopias (in the generic sense) demonstrate the impossibility of utopia rather than represent its establishment or existence. In short, the spaces and times of modern narrative forms involve critical-historicist operations that distinguish outside from inside, important from unimportant, now from then, here from there, all in the name of meaning. Meaning may in fact simply refer to a limited part cut from an unlimited whole. To wit, "everywhere" and "always," or "earth" and "4.5 billion years," do not serve meaning making so much as destroy its possibility.[20] The new weird, along with cultural geology, suggests this unlimited whole by refusing to allow the whole to be brought under control by history or critique.

The novel as a form involves these limitations as a matter of course. Ghosh reveals the challenges this form thus presents to those who would represent the Anthropocene; in the course of his discussion of setting, he provides a means for understanding the Veniss milieu as something other than a delimited time and space that serves as a container of meaning at a human scale. Ghosh may not be a cultural geologist in the strictest sense if by this term we designate, following McGurl, someone who positions "culture in a time-frame large enough to crack open the carapace of human self-concern, exposing it to the idea, and maybe even the fact, of its external ontological preconditions, its ground."[21] Rather than exposing the human for the sake of doing so, which often seems the intention of those who practice cultural geology, Ghosh aspires to a more obviously political practice that serves humanity even as he recognizes the constitutive limitations of this practice. Thus his interest with the limitations of the novel and setting begin and end with marginalized groups and individuals already exposed to the materiality of the world by way of the overdeveloped world's lack of concern for them.

Nonetheless, Ghosh demonstrates how humanist forms of discourse and representation, such as the novel, include in their assumptions the same critical and historicist notions that produce the Anthropocene itself, if on a smaller scale, and thus his work fits well with that of McGurl, Dipesh Chakrabarty, Timothy Clark, Bruno Latour, and others who seek to rethink the relationship of the human to the earth. That said, in Ghosh's argument, the novel as a form has difficulty describing and narrativizing the extension and duration of the Anthropocene precisely because it makes meaning by way of drawing boundaries around heres and nows, and ignoring the unbounded (in anthropocentric terms) space and time of the planet in which the Anthropocene takes place.

The meaning-making trope or device called setting is not simply a noun that refers to time and place. It is also an action, an operation, by which time and place are established as vehicles for or containers of meaning.

Ghosh contrasts the discontinuities we find in the novel, the modern form of prose narrative par excellence, with the "boundless time and space that are conjured up by other forms of prose narrative" such as epic and myth.[22] Such earlier forms move through the vastness of nonanthropocentric time and space with ease, likely because their meanings accrue according to nonmodern knowledge practices and without specific regard for humanity. Ghosh asserts, "Novels, on the other hand, conjure up worlds that become real because of their finitude and distinctiveness. Within the mansions of serious fiction, no one will speak of how the continents were created; nor will they refer to the passage of thousands of years: connections and events on this scale appear not just unlikely but also absurd within the delimited horizon of a novel."[23] Of course, novels assume mountain formation, coastline erosion, and the timescales at which such events take place, just as modern knowledge practices generally assume the materiality that conditions the possibility of their very existence and transformation over time. However, the Anthropocene urgently establishes the need to rethink knowledge by demonstrating that the stable condition that affords it—the earth itself—is revealed to be stable only when considered as an index to human being and its extraordinarily short (in geologic terms) temporality. As Ghosh goes on to note, "The earth of the Anthropocene is precisely a world of insistent, inescapable discontinuities, animated by forces that are nothing if not inconceivably vast."[24] In short, the vastness of these forces calls into question any possibility of "setting" the time or space in which they are felt.

Setting involves a materiality that recedes from the immediate heres and nows produced by the novel, a process the Veniss milieu reverses by way of actively receding setting, as I will discuss below. For now, suffice it to say that the discontinuities Ghosh describes create an apparent isolation for a given novel's setting, narrative, and meaning. These discontinuities, even as they force the larger world to recede, nonetheless assume a relationship with other spaces and times by way of potential physical or temporal travel, communication, or both. Characters isolated in a given place can walk, drive, sail, or fly to other places. Characters isolated in a given time can wait for another time, archive their thoughts for future consideration, or discover similarly archived thoughts from the past. (All of this is to say nothing about devices, such as prolepsis and analepsis, by which novelists meaningfully relate one moment to another.) Thus the discontinuities that produce settings are only ever constructions. Setting manifests only insofar as a critical operation produces it as such in willful and necessary ignorance of the larger material world out of which it is cut.

Ghosh writes, "Since each setting is particular to itself, its connections to the world beyond are inevitably *made to recede* (as, for example, the imperial networks that make possible the worlds portrayed by Jane Austen and Charlotte Brontë)."[25] Ghosh's parenthetical statement is telling insofar as it suggests Edward Said's groundbreaking argument about the function of empire and colonialism in Austen's *Mansfield Park* (1814). Said argues that the existence of Mansfield Park, the estate, requires Sir Thomas Bertram's (and by extension England's) exploitation of Antigua and similarly colonized places. Despite the novel's implicit acknowledgment that Mansfield Park relies on Antigua and its resources for its very existence, the peripheral, colonized space is infrequently acknowledged and never seen. For Said, the novel's "very odd combination of casualness and stress" reveals Austen "to be *assuming* (just as Fanny assumes, in both senses of the word) the importance of an empire to the situation at home."[26] In other words, yes, other places do in fact recede from a novel's proper setting, but they do so only in a limited, subjective sense. To whatever degree setting relies on discontinuities in space and time, it relies on an abstraction produced by human artifice. This artifice, the production of selective or constructed end points rather than the use of natural ones that exceed human perception, allows fiction to achieve a certain truth.[27] Fanny Price and the rest at Mansfield Park may be able to forget about Antigua and Sir Thomas's concerns there consciously or subjectively because they only rarely, if ever, perceive that place or those concerns. However—and here we come to the crux of the matter—they can never forget about them materially or objectively, no matter how set they are. Their material connection to these other places not only makes possible the artificial discontinuity called setting, but also grounds the norms and manners they live by, a point Said has already made in reference to a description of Sir Thomas's return to Mansfield Park from Antigua:

> More clearly than anywhere else in her fiction, Austen here synchronizes domestic with international authority, making it plain that the values associated with such higher things as ordination, law, and propriety must be grounded firmly in actual rule over and possession of territory. She sees clearly that to hold and rule Mansfield Park is to hold and rule an imperial estate in close, not to say inevitable association with it.[28]

As such, we see that materiality cuts through setting regardless of the human's attempts to isolate itself and its concerns. The Anthropocene is the knife by which the materiality of the earth cuts through anthropocentrism and anthropomorphism. It is what no amount of critique or history can deny as the planet grows increasingly hostile to not only human life but also to human self-perception.

The issue of setting is not, to Ghosh, merely interesting. Said's argument demonstrates the political stakes that setting involves, and Ghosh pushes these political stakes in new directions when he discusses the issue in the context of the Anthropocene. Following from this discussion, he notes, "The Anthropocene has reversed the temporal order of modernity: those at the margins are now the first to experience the future that awaits all of us."[29] As Rob Nixon has argued, there is an "environmentalism of the poor," of people who experience the "slow violence" of climate change and who seem to be beyond help for the fact that what they experience resists popular forms of representation.[30] These poor, mainly located in the underdeveloped world and the global south, now have the "privilege" of being a geocultural or geopolitical vanguard, where this prefix is synonymous with the "geo-" in Timothy Murphy's formulation of geoliterature, a literature more of earth and its materiality than of the earth and its abstract lines.[31] This vanguard witnesses the future arrive in the form of rising sea levels, record temperature spikes, and disappearing biomass, even as a different but related future arrives in the overdeveloped world in the form of the remainder of carbon energy and the next generation of smartphone extracted from the labor of those beyond setting. These individuals and groups are subject not to a cognitive estrangement by which they discover their differences vis-à-vis those who precede them historically. Rather, they confront a fantastic materiality that conditions them without being known or knowable according to the humanist assumptions that produced it—humanist assumptions that have always already failed to represent them and their interests.

Thus, the solution to the problem of representation Nixon reveals is not a new setting or a shift to another discontinuity in space and time now centered at or within the former periphery. If the poor of underdeveloped nations experience the Anthropocene first, and if they only ever exist beyond the horizon that is the boundary of setting, what form of representation could suffice? Although Gayatri Chakravorty Spivak no longer tells us that the subaltern cannot speak, she nonetheless makes clear the difficulty of representing the voices of those who exist beyond the margins of imperial centers. If someone speaks for the subaltern, then the subaltern is not speaking. If the subaltern speaks and thus becomes capable of representing herself, then she is no longer subaltern, or has at least begun the process of joining hegemonic discourse.[32] Similarly, to become a subject capable of speaking, a nonsubject must gain access to a setting, to a delimited time and place that provides a container and vehicle for meaning accessible in one fashion or another to others similarly situated. Such a time and space cannot be Antigua as viewed from Mansfield Park qua Antigua as viewed from the setting Mansfield Park in the novel *Mansfield Park*. The fact of setting presupposes the fact of subjectivity, and subjectivity presupposes setting. Each separately and both together presuppose the anthropocentric and anthropomorphic meaning that makes representing the Anthropocene, and that of those most affected by it, impossible.

Such is the case because once we accept setting as a condition of our fictions and therefore the recession of the larger world out of which setting is cut, we accept all that comes with and follows from it:

representation, history, critique. Settings are produced once and for all so long as these other concepts—which maintain the visibility, intelligibility, and integrity of settings as well as their social and political force—continue to operate. Even if a setting is undermined in some way, even if it is shown to be a construction of human artifice, its legacy remains in the historical record and flows forward in time. The Veniss milieu, a total space with no center and a time that short-circuits directionality and causality, refuses such production and the anthropocentric or anthropomorphic forces thereof. Even if the nonhuman, material forces it does involve continue to affect human beings, they can neither be scaled to human dimensions nor indexed to human concerns. Rather, they cause the humanistic notion of setting itself to recede toward a midpoint between no other terms, allowing the milieu's middle placeness to expand and fill extension and duration. The Veniss milieu suggests a weird space and time that no longer produces anything like what we now call meaning.

REFUGEES IN THE WEIRD HERE AND NOW

"Balzac's War" is of the last Veniss texts, and it is also the last to make clear reference to events that took place in the actual city called Veniss. It does not reference the city by name, although it does reference Veniss's sister city, Balthakazar. (It is also the last of these texts to make this reference.) It begins with two characters, Balzac and Jamie, wandering through the ruins of the latter city, where there is nothing left of the humanity it once possessed:

> Husks and shells, as dead as the hollowed-out, mummified
> corpses of tortoises and jackals after a drought: the idea
> of "city" stripped down to its most fundamental elements,
> the superfluous flourishes of paint, writing, road signs,
> windows, scoured away in an effort to reveal the unadorned
> and beautifully harsh truth. Gutted weapons embankments
> pointed towards the sky, but could not defend the city from the
> true enemy.[33]

These ruins do not authorize a romanticized, ironic melancholy; nor do they permit a chance to reflect on the falleness of greatness past, such as we find, for example, in Shelley's "Ozymandias" (1818). No one speaks from beyond the grave to express anthropocentric power, hubris, or self-regard. Jamie states, as she looks at a pile of bones, "My father says no one knows what did this. If these are just old graves opened by the sands or if something killed them all off. . . . Whatever happened, happened a long time ago. There's nothing to be done for them."[34] She senses that the city represents some past and lost human achievement, but there is no statue of a former ruler to demand future generations despair as they look on his works. Moreover, there is no memory of such a ruler, or even of rulers in general. There is no mention of soliminds, the Social Revolutions, or anything about the world before the crèches or of the people who lived in that world. The weapons embankments were once likely pointed at living things (although inhuman living things), but the enemy they could never defeat is an encroaching milieu that exposes all human attempts at order as the limited and limiting devices they are.

During their exploration of Balthakazar's ruins, Jamie and Balzac discover what appears to be a dead flesh dog. In the final pages of the story, narrated after the reader knows what their fates will be, the two remark that the body reminds them of something they might have read about in "the old books." As they do so, the flesh dog's body splits open to reveal something else: "They heard a leathery, cracking sound and the flesh dog's bulbous forehead split open and out struggled a creature the size of a man's heart. It glistened with moisture and, seeming to grow larger, spread its blue-black wings over the ruins of the flesh. It had all the delicate and alien allure of a damselfly."[35] The creature, whose beauty they are attracted to even as it signals their eventual destruction, flies away. They imagine that it must be a messenger or a beacon, although for what they cannot guess. The reader by this point already understands: the creature will alert the meerkats living below the remains of Veniss (or whatever authority exists there by this point) of the return of humans to Balthakazar and precipitate an invasion of flesh dogs. This invasion, one aspect of the war to which the story's title refers, will cost both Jamie and Balzac their lives. She dies twice, once at the hands of the flesh dogs and again after her head is attached to a flesh dog and her hybrid form is shot by Balzac's brother, Jeffer. Balzac merely dies once. As he attempts to save his lover's head and take it to the meerkats, who might be able to save it, he is shot by a fellow human in an act of futile species self-defense. Such a death—one of which there can be no memory whatsoever, one that stands in contrast to the inhuman memories possessed by those grafted to the flesh dogs—is perhaps the only victory left to a doomed humanity.

"Balzac's War" dramatizes the peculiar discontinuity endemic to the Veniss milieu, a weird discontinuity that does not cut a specific time and place from a larger world that is made to recede as the result of this operation, but rather one that forces setting itself, and its attendant concepts of delimited time and space, to recede. During the battle in which flesh dog Jamie returns to haunt Balzac, Jeffer thinks over what it means to live in the milieu: "They were refugees fleeing the past, and their best strategy had proved to be the simplest: in the unraveling of their lives to forget, to disremember, to exist purely in the *now*."[36] Jeffer, Balzac, Jamie, and the other inhabitants of the milieu have no account of the past, no history from which they may flee knowingly, as do modern humans who seek to differentiate themselves from a primitive or innocent premodernity. In the context of Jeffer's contemplation of the past, he and Balzac are fleeing from Jamie and from Balzac's relationship with her, but more generally, the past implied by the ruins of Balthakazar does not constitute a knowable history to these refugees and can provide no previous setting from which to differentiate themselves. Their status as refugees connects them to the refugees of the late twentieth and early twenty-first centuries who flee without always understanding the processes that brought about the conditions from which they flee, especially when these conditions involve catastrophic climate change. Just as for Ghosh the underdeveloped world becomes a vanguard, the first to experience a future created by forces highly resistant to the mechanisms of representation, the remnants of humanity in "Balzac's War," fighting their last fight in the ruins of a city of which they have no personal or cultural memory, experience a threat approaching them from a future they cannot understand as the consequence of a past they cannot perceive.

They are thus left in a radical now, with no future and no past in the conventional sense and thus no capacity for ordering according to historicist or critical operations.

The best Balzac, Jamie, and the rest can do is recall the old books. However, these books contain stories whose capacity for historicism, or even mimeticism, cannot be verified. These books likely include a few stories with which readers of the Veniss cycle, who must themselves constantly navigate texts of various representational levels, will be familiar. "The Sea, Mendeho, and Moonlight" may well be found in such books, as it seems to narrate an actual event taking place in the milieu and operates as myth told among the inhabitants of the milieu—a myth quietly endorsed by the soliminds as a means to maintain their power. "Jessible and the Metal Dragon," a fragment for VanderMeer's readers, narrates events that may or may not have taken place in the milieu. More importantly, however, it also exists as a book in "A Heart for Lucretia," where it is known as *The Metal Dragon and Jessible*. Gerard reads this book to Lucretia, and because he fails to understand it as a fable and instead takes it to be truthful, he allows it to guide his doomed quest to save his twin sister.

"A Heart for Lucretia" itself seems to be a tale developed and told in the Veniss milieu, one that mythologizes the origins of the flesh dogs that come to plague the remnants of humanity in "Balzac's War." It thus "explains" the gap in history implied by the ruins of Balthakazar that Jamie and Balzac confront—an explanation no mimetic, modern form of narrative can produce. VanderMeer himself refers to "A Heart for Lucretia" as a sort of myth: "I imagined myself as a storyteller in the year 12,000 AD writing a story about the year 11,500 AD. Thus can the mythic coincide with the science fictional."[37] As Ghosh might note, such mythopoesis does not participate in the operations of setting. Rather than make clear and causal connections among various delimited moments in time, myth takes place in a nonhuman time whose ordering is impossible by anthropocentric standards and thus incapable of providing meaning for humanity, even if it provides explanation (which will always be dubious according to historicist and critical thought).

The Book of the City, a fictional text in "Three Days in a Border Town," may be even more indicative of the problematic nature of recorded history in the milieu than any of the previously mentioned texts. As the protagonist of the story, a nameless woman, searches for the city that may or may not have taken her husband, she writes about her object of desire in a blank book she acquired at some point in the course of her quest. Although it seems that she records stories about the city offered by other people, it may also be the case that she constructs her own stories. Regardless of the questionable nature of what she records, she treats what she then reads in the book as absolute fact. At one point she wonders, with regard to a strange funeral procession she has just witnessed, "What does it mean? Is it something you need to write down in your book?"[38] In the next paragraph, VanderMeer writes, "In *The Book of the City* it is written," with the passive voice seeming to grant an impersonal factuality, perhaps even a truth, to all that the book records for the woman as she reads what she has written. Elsewhere in "Three Days in a Border Town," the woman sees children playing with old holographic devices that project images "of an m'kat and a fleshdog," clearly connecting the story (and by extension "The City," to which I turn momentarily) to the Veniss milieu. However, these "harbingers of the past," these "ghosts with the very real ability to inflict harm," do nothing to describe the specific events through which the world became this way, do nothing to define what the city actually is beyond a desire and/or a mirage, do nothing to describe a mechanism of causality that explains the forces that govern history in the milieu.[39]

The references to meerkats and flesh dogs alongside references to familiars in the final Veniss text do not overcome the problem of setting described heretofore. The penultimate installment of the Veniss cycle, "The City," pushes the resistance to setting found in "Balzac's War" and other Veniss texts to such an extreme that, short of a strict narrativization of the events and mechanisms that brought the world to this state, nothing could suffice to set the milieu. Likely such a narrativization could only come from a source external to the milieu, such as VanderMeer himself, meaning that the milieu will always remain fundamentally unset according to its internal logic. "The City" thus serves as the best means by which we might grasp the fundamental uncertainties of the Veniss milieu. There are no clear references in "The City" to anything that clearly belongs to Veniss. The city for which its characters long resembles the

Veniss or Balthakazar familiar to the reader from other texts in the series, and the desert through which they wander resembles the one Shadrach once traveled through and Gerard once crossed, but only insofar as words like "city" and "desert" conjure abstractions that might relate to any number of concrete entities. Nothing in the story confirms such specificity. VanderMeer writes that "The City" could be "the ultimate far-future story, possibly the end result of the *Veniss Underground* milieu. But, in a sense, it hardly matters whether the setting is fantastic or futuristic."[40] The insignificance VanderMeer assigns to this question demonstrates the degree to which the Veniss texts dispose of the conventional discontinuities in time and space termed "setting." In "The City," all we are left with is a marginal desert that possesses neither duration nor extension in any anthropomorphic or anthropocentric sense.

The short story is divided into three parts, the first and third of which are entitled "The Detective." The second part, internally divided into six sections, is entitled "The Accounts of Others." The story begins when the eponymous detective of Parts 1 and 3 discovers an apparently murdered rabbit wearing a waistcoat and carrying a pocket watch. The detective is connected to a familiar, a manta ray–like parasite (or, less likely, symbiote) wired into the detective's central nervous system by an ethereal umbilical cord. The familiar feeds the detective memories, including memories of Lewis Carrol's *Alice's Adventures in Wonderland* (1865), in an effort to familiarize the detective with her situation in a way that will pacify her and allow the familiar to continue in its relationship with her.[41] Part of this familiarization involves projecting to the detective (and later other characters) images of a city at which no one can ever arrive and which no two people even agree exists. At the conclusion of Part 1, the rabbit wakes up and tells the detective that it is not dead, that the detective is "the broken one," and that the rabbit has been sent to "solve" her.[42]

Part 2's six sections seem to be narrated by other inhabitants of the desert in which the detective has found the rabbit. Each section describes the relationship between someone and the city. For each narrator, the city appears as a mirage. Rather than a memory or coherent idea, the city seems to be a projection of some ineffable desire or, more likely, a false recognition implanted into individuals by familiars as a means to make the milieu more human, more familiar, and therefore less threatening to basic tenets of human being, such as setting. One of the narrators states, "There was nothing to stop me from getting there." However, as this narrator goes on to explain, "The desert spread out ahead of me, the city where it had always been: in front of me. It never changed. It always seemed to be in the same place: a dark glitter, a black speck in the corner of my eye. A hint of a scent, taken by the wind. I never made any progress toward it. It never made any progress toward me. You could say we were equals in a way."[43] At the end of this account, the narrator states,

> Eventually, I begged the city to accept me. I stood there and begged for this dot at the corner of my vision to let me get close.
>
> But by then it was too late. By then its absence had become too familiar.[44]

After several more narrators relate their own, likely simulated, experiences with the city (or, in some cases, the simulated experiences of others as they have heard them), the story returns to the detective, still in conversation with the rabbit. The rabbit again tells the detective that she is the broken one, not the corpse she has been sent to solve. The rabbit asks the detective if she even wants to return to the city. When the detective states that she does not, the rabbit says that she should then not be afraid to give up her manta ray–like familiar. When the detective then does so, the rabbit reveals itself to be yet another familiar and takes control of her. The story's last lines read: "By what right should I have achieved this state? By what right should I never solve my case, only to have it solve me?"[45]

The detective's solution at the hands of the rabbit has to do with making the desert, an inhuman place without any discernible boundaries and thus granting no meaning, familiar. The image of the city as a specific place, a specific setting, serves to accomplish this task, to grant to the human detective the possibility of such meaning. The detective, however, has been too broken by her experience in the desert and thus no longer desires setting. The rabbit reveals itself as a familiar in order to solve this problem and return the human to her pacified existence. Importantly, this plotline echoes one found in "Detectives and Cadavers" in which that story's eponymous detective, during the first of the assaults that will eventually drive humanity from Veniss, kills the "muttie" he had been sent to solve. As the creature, which seems to be a sort of proto–flesh dog, dies, it tells the detective, "You kill . . . You kill Funnyyy," in reference to the so-called Funny People, individuals apparently naturally born with defects such as missing limbs, with which it had aligned itself and whom the humans euthanize. The detective, stunned by the creature's speech, continues to try to kill it even as he questions those who had told him that such creatures possessed no such capability, and thus no humanity or value. The last words the creature speaks in the story are: "Weee makkk . . . Wee makkk you . . ."[46] On the one hand, the beast's last words suggest, in a Foucauldian way, the manner in which those who would call themselves normal produce abnormality as a means by which to negatively define themselves. On the other hand, and more importantly, these words, taken with the detective's solution in "The City," further suggest how the Veniss milieu undoes the types of discontinuities characteristic of setting. The detective of "Detective and Cadavers" is the first in Veniss to experience the future—an inhuman future dominated by nonhuman agencies and forces comprising nonnatural life forms whose origins might be traceable to a human agent but whose evolutions cannot be made to mean in any human sense. These evolutions take place underground, beyond the margins of human setting. Even as they materially affect setting, they nonetheless resist its embrace. In short, they engulf setting and create a milieu.

Although the desert and the receding city of "The City" are the outcomes of a series of destructive events, the revelation at the end of story is not an apocalypse. It does not uncover any deeper, concealed, human truth about the Veniss milieu. At the story's conclusion, readers have no information about why the familiars do what they do, how they came to dominate humanity, what happened to the meerkats or flesh dogs, or even if any of the past events of the Veniss milieu took place. Just as Nicholas's and Shadrach's failures to know Veniss do not indicate any shortcoming in them, this absence of information does not imply any lack on the part of the narrators, any omission on VanderMeer's part, or any incomprehension on the part of readers. Rather, "The City" represents an amplification of the milieu's resistance to setting and all of its attendant concerns with the discontinuities and delimitations that produce meaning at anthropocentric scales. A resistance already at work in previous texts in the narrative achieves its final form here, a finality that even the subsequent Veniss text, "Three Days in a Border Town," cannot overcome. Playing on the conventional human need for bounded spaces and times, the familiars (or even the desert itself as the producer of mirage) entice human beings with images of a city that never centers itself in their field of vision, and neither arrives nor can be arrived at.

Likewise, playing on readerly expectations for settings, VanderMeer offers "The City" as an apparent final state for the Veniss narrative. "Three Days in a Border Town" demonstrates how things may continue to happen in the milieu, but that the milieu itself can never be set and thereby become a ground for human meaning. To be clear: such an end point should provide closure for the narrative and therefore the possibility of meaning. However, neither the city nor "The City" ever becomes a stable point on which the detective or other narrators, or readers of the Veniss narrative, can ground themselves. The city only exists as an apparent setting, a possible setting, a nigh setting; it is a false middle in the midst of a middle place. It only ever recedes, leaving in its wake the formerly marginalized and forgotten material world that previously existed beyond human concern even as it conditioned humanity's every action and thought. As one of the story's narrators puts it, "People in the city had lost the thread of living without familiars. People there had just lost the thread, period. Deep wired into the spinal cord. Sucking into them. Sucking out of them. A city of spines. A city of familiars. A city of people. A city of not-people. Had it created them or had they created it?"[47] Thus the Veniss milieu solves the problem of representing the sort of inhuman force the Anthropocene reveals, but this solution involves something other than longer narratives, bigger spaces, or vaster periods of time. Likewise, the solution here is not about telescoping between the large and the small; nor is it strictly a reconfiguration of subjectivity in terms of one flavor or another of posthumanism, although such reconfig-uration may occur and posthumanism may be a reciprocal consequence of living in a milieu. The Veniss milieu recedes setting and thereby offers a larger, less contained or containable world in which the human can only ever be entangled in a collectivity, equal to the city as one more open, blurry-edged thing situated between no beginning and no ending. Rather than solving the mystery of the city (or "The City"), the human (or reader) is solved by way of eliminating the delimitations that produce and afford its humanity (or that allow for meaning).

3

NO ONE
MAKES IT OUT,
THERE MAY
BE A WAY

AMBERGRIS AS
WORDS AND WORLD

AMBERGRIS, WORLDS, AND WORDS

Janice Shriek's biography of her heterodox historian brother, Duncan Shriek, originally conceived as an afterword to Duncan's *The Hoegbotton Guide to the Early History of Ambergris*, begins with an anecdote about another historian, Duncan's former student, lover, and, later, archrival, Mary Sabon: "Mary Sabon once said of my brother Duncan Shriek that 'He is not a human being at all, but composed entirely of digressions and transgressions.'"[1] Duncan is perhaps the most persistent character in Ambergris, the only one to play a significant role in all three of the Ambergris novels: *City of Saints and Madmen*, *Shriek: An Afterword*, and *Finch*.[2] However, the nature of his appearances in these novels, which is to say how he manifests rather than what he accomplishes, demonstrates how these novels complicate the various and varied relationships between material world and immaterial text established in and assumed by experimental contemporary fiction and generic fantasy.

In *City of Saints and Madmen,* a novel comprising many disparate fragments and narratives in a recognizably postmodernist manner, Duncan appears only as the author of the aforementioned guide. The conditions under which he writes the *Guide,* and its ideal and actual audiences, prove to be serious constraints for Duncan as an historian and a writer. As Janice puts it, "Serious journals do not review travel guides and tourists rarely remember who wrote them."[3] Duncan distinguishes himself from the guide and from the rest of *City of Saints and Madmen,* into which so many authors (including Jeff VanderMeer) dissolve and disappear, through his use of voluminous, polemical footnotes. These footnotes refer to people and events of which the reader will know little but clearly mean a great deal (in terms of significance and personal interest) to him. This apparent idiosyncrasy notwithstanding, he seems to remain in *City of Saints and Madmen* an entirely textual being, one who exists as a sort of author function on the one hand and as a reaction to textuality on the other.

In *Shriek: An Afterword,* which begins with Janice's anecdote about Sabon, Duncan's textual being remains operational and his common refrain, "No one makes it out," comes to refer to this condition as it is conventionally understood by those bound to representationalist and textualist logics. Duncan seems to distinguish himself from the text in which he appears, one written and edited and thus largely controlled by someone else, only through paratextual intervention: interpolated, parenthetical commentary that responds, in Nabakovian fashion, to Janice's representations and interpretations of his life.

In *Finch*—in which Duncan manifests first as an apparently dead body, then as a memory experienced by someone to whom it does not belong, and finally as a distinct and living body constructed from someone else's flesh—he emerges from textuality as defined by others. This emergence comes as the result of a textuality–materiality that Duncan discovers, deploys, and comes to embody. Mary Sabon will turn out to be wrong about so many things by the time *Shriek* has concluded, including her assessment of Duncan. He only appears as digression and transgression insofar as others represent him and insofar as these representations allow him to respond in a textual manner. However, these responses are for the benefit of those who cannot understand what he becomes: a being who falls into the spaces between the words, and who in so falling binds these words together as a material world, an example of VanderMeer's fantastic materiality.

Janice spends much of her account of Duncan's life digressing. She seems to have an explanation for and a description of the consequences of Sabon's insult and a desire to relate this explanation to the reader. However, she also seems only capable of proceeding by constantly pausing and restarting her narration. She writes, for example, "I really ought to start again, though. Begin afresh," "Now I should start again," "Can I start again? Will you let me start again?," "Time to start over. Another dead white page to fill with dead black type, so I'll fill it. Why not?," and so on.[4] One example of Janice's digressive style, with which she begins the fifth chapter of her manuscript and introduces an anecdote about her childhood with Duncan, starts to render the outlines and stakes of the Ambergris novels visible: "Can a childhood memory be misconstrued as starting over? I don't think so. Not if I tell it this way."[5] Janice goes on to describe how, while playing in the yard of their childhood home in the city of Stockton, Duncan sets out into the thick forest adjacent to this yard. In an early example of the precociousness and iconoclasm that would come to define him, and that would cause his downfall later in life, he insists to Janice, "We need to go exploring. No more paths. We don't need paths."[6] Janice follows him. She revels in being led, in abdicating her role as the elder sibling, if only for a moment: "A part of me could have kept going on hour after hour, with no end in sight, and been satisfied with that uncertainty."[7] In one of his interpellations to Janice's manuscript, marked by curly brackets, Duncan responds, "{Then you know how I have felt my entire adult life—except we are told there is no uncertainty. *No one makes it out*, we're told, from birth until our deathbed, in a thousand spoken and unspoken ways. It's just a matter of when and where—and if I could discover the truth in the meantime.}"[8]

Duncan borrows what will become for him and the text a refrain, "No one makes it out," from Samuel Tonsure, a monk who participated in the settlement of Ambergris; stood by as the settlers claimed the lives of countless gray caps (who had previously settled the area); eventually disappeared in the underworld below the city; and may in the end be Duncan himself. Tonsure wrote "No one makes it out" on the last page of his journal, a page lost to history (and which never appears in the Ambergris materials). It references being trapped in the hallucinogenic, fungal world of the gray caps hidden beneath Ambergris as well as the certainty of the end of existence at death. However, as I shall demonstrate here, it also refers to what seems to be a nigh-carceral textual condition, one assumed by nearly all of the inhabitants of Ambergris and one that poses the gravest threat to their existence. Writing of this condition on the final page of her manuscript, Janice puts it this way: "There's a space between each word that I can't help but fall into, and these spaces are as wide as the words and twice as treacherous."[9] Janice's disappearance, and her failure to reappear in *Finch* except as the writer of *Shriek: An Afterword*, suggest the dangers to be found in textuality. If we read *Shriek* as a postmodernist novel, the spaces between the words adumbrate an infinite regress, a bottomless pit of signification threatening to swallow even the primary world in which the reader reads. By contrast, if we also read the novel as fantasy, one set in a secondary world or an otherworld beyond the primary world and the logics governing it, then we might find something else in the space Janice describes, something Duncan comes to see and make use of: an impossible material condition we do not share and therefore cannot intuit, much less inhabit—one grounded on textuality itself.

VanderMeer's use of postmodernist, textualist poetics as well as the world building and impossibility characteristic of genre fantasy oppose one another according to conventional understandings of each. However, if we read Ambergris in the context of both, then we discover something altogether different: a materiality not opposed to textuality but one based on it, a materiality and textuality that are one and the same thing.

This fantastic materiality, and the threat it poses to textualist and representationalist understandings of the world, becomes visible near the conclusion of *Shriek*, when Janice finally confronts Mary Sabon. Sabon has dedicated her career to opposing Duncan's work, insisting that Ambergris conforms to her theories about it despite her knowledge to the contrary (a knowledge she disavows). Once upon a time, Duncan had exposed Sabon to the materiality overlaying Ambergris as it is seen and experienced by nearly everyone who inhabits the city, a materiality created and imposed by the gray caps, a mysterious species of fungal beings whom Duncan respects and fears for their capacity to bend materiality to their will and whom Sabon represents as unintelligent animals. After Sabon insults Duncan, Janice slaps her face and states, "Once upon a time [. . .] no one knew your name. Someday no one will again."[10] At the moment of this confrontation, Janice has lost any power she ever wielded in Ambergris as the foremost prophet, and profiteer, of the so-called New Art. Yet her words will prove themselves to be true. Mary Sabon's name never appears in *Finch*, the final Ambergris novel. By contrast, Duncan will emerge there as a being of impossible material dimensions. He will emerge as someone no longer constrained by a textuality bound to a materiality outside of itself that the textuality can only hope to represent. He will emerge as someone who has found a way to inhabit textuality as a material condition that retains the malleability of text.

Given the power Duncan comes to inhabit and wield—the power to create the world rather than simply reflect it—what Janice does to Sabon becomes more important than what she says to Sabon. Janice possesses not only words but also the pair of glasses her brother once used on Sabon. These glasses force their wearer to see beyond the humanist, textualist, representationalist assumptions under which Ambergris lives— assumptions concealing the horror of the fungal world with which the wearer is always already unknowingly involved. They reveal an invisible film of materiality clinging to everything in Ambergris, the evidence for which Sabon has dedicated her career to denying. Janice describes Sabon's reaction to having them forced on her:

> Mary was staring at me as the scales of the lenses filled with
> that amazing blackness—and she began to scream as soon
> as the top half of her pupils disappeared, a scream that grew

deeper and more desperate as it continued, and continued.
It was as if she had forgotten she could close her eyes. All she
had to do was close her eyes, and, after a time, I began to wish
she *would* close her eyes.

She stumbled, caught herself, blinked twice, stopped
screaming—but, no: she was still screaming, it was just
soundless. A look had come over her that destroyed the unity
between mouth, eyes, forehead, cheekbones. Before me, she
became undone looking through those glasses.[11]

Sabon sees Ambergris as it is, beyond anthropocentric claims and
assumptions. The city and its materiality are quite different than what
she wishes they might be, or what in her scholarship she insists they
must be. (When Janice is exposed to Ambergris as it is, she responds:
"What I am trying to say is that the real world, the world I had known
for over fifty years, no longer held true when confronted by this other
world that existed on top of it but also within it." With regard to Sabon,
Janice writes, "All of her scholarship, all of her will, would be focused on
making what she had seen as unreal, as distant, as possible."[12]) Sabon
denies the role played by the gray caps in Ambergris's history, which
Duncan studied and publicized, and which once manifested, centuries
earlier, in a holocaust in which nearly the entire population of the city
disappeared. This materiality undermines textuality; it resists attempts
to make it mean according to anthropocentric and anthropomorphic
techniques and desires even as it exists only as a consequence of a textuality produced by a writer named Jeff VanderMeer. The Ambergris novels thus produce a world and condition that their postmodernist poetics
would normally deny but here serve to ground. How do these novels
begin as text and end as materiality? To borrow Duncan's final words
to his sister, which respond to the assertion that "no one makes it out":
"There may be a way."[13]

To better understand the problematic the Ambergris novels develop
and engage, we must return to the respective fates of Mary Sabon and
Duncan Shriek. As stated, Mary Sabon—despite her importance to
Ambergris, despite her eminence as the historian of the city, despite

being someone beloved not only by academics but also by people in general, despite being someone whose intellectual abilities and academic credentials are matched only by her physical beauty—disappears from Ambergris with the conclusion of *Shriek: An Afterword*. She falls into the spaces between the words as the representations supporting her existence disappear, or as they lose whatever force they once possessed. By contrast, in *Finch*, Duncan emerges from the constraints textuality had seemed to impose on him in the previous two novels to play a vital role in the revolution against the gray caps that begins there. Sabon's historicism and criticality—which assert how things must be this way because it cannot imagine them to be another way, whose condition is a materiality they unknowingly rely on and claim to represent but ultimately cannot face—allow her to make her life meaningful.

Duncan flees from this humanist condition. Through his escape, by finding a way (both a technique and a path), he manifests as a material being, in contrast to the immaterial and textual being readers may have assumed him to be before *Finch*. Thus, the final Ambergris novel subverts the apparently postmodernist poetics at work in the previous two novels and reveals them as part and parcel of a world-building exercise rather than a world-critiquing one. *Finch* alone among these novels is authored solely by Jeff VanderMeer and describes characters who rarely, if ever, address their participation in a narrative or how their lives are mediated by the formal capacities of the novel or genre fiction—which is to say that *Finch* seems to prioritize its mimetic capacities rather than its textual ones. However, far from rejecting the experimental textuality of the previous two novels, it weirdly affirms it, although in an entirely unexpected way: as materiality itself. Of course, *Finch* and the rest of the Ambergris novels describe a world that not only does not exist but that remains wholly fantastic vis-à-vis the world in which the reader reads.[14] As such, Ambergris must be understood as an example of a secondary world or an otherworld of the sort found in conventional fantasy, and it thus must be understood to oppose itself to the bottomless textuality and cynical criticality characteristic of so much postmodernist fiction.

Duncan Shriek's manifestation in *Finch*, out of the textuality of the previous two Ambergris novels and as the result of a complex, fantastic,

even grotesque technique of memory on the part of the novel's eponymous detective, serves as a means by which to grasp the overall importance of the Ambergris novels. These novels reject conventional notions
of textuality by affirming the capacities of such textuality to create a
world whose existence depends entirely on textual descriptions of it.
Thus they provide another example of fantastic materiality. If the Veniss
texts' milieu undermines setting and thereby challenge the anthropocentric and anthropomorphic discontinuities required by meaning, the
Ambergris novels draw the imaginary worlds of genre fiction into a relationship with the textual experimentation associated with postmodernist fiction. In doing so, the Ambergris novels expose how these worlds
and how this form of textuality maintain humanist assumptions about
representation and reality even as they demonstrate how the new weird
and cultural geology might overcome these assumptions.

The present chapter takes the following form.[15] First, I will elaborate on the tension I have briefly described here, one as central to the
Ambergris novels as it is unexpected and productive. On the one hand,
these novels deploy a postmodernist, textualist poetics, which in previous deployments call into question the material world in which they
appear. On the other hand, these novels make use of a certain convention
of genre fantasy, the secondary world, and thus assert the sort of naive
materiality postmodernist poetics often takes to task. This admixture
produces startling effects, namely an excessive textuality *cum* materiality that overcomes first the shortcomings of naive materialities opposed
to textuality and second the shortcomings of textuality by which any
ground for further thought is destroyed except the material one that textuality cannot acknowledge. John Clute's development of the grammar
of story and Brian McHale's seminal argument about the ontological
poetics of postmodernist fiction provide the basis for my argument. This
discussion allows us to understand the Ambergris novels, taken together,
as a peculiar example of what Mitchum Heuhls calls the posttheory theory novel, a recent development in contemporary fiction that, knowingly
or otherwise, makes use of techniques and conventions associated with
a certain historical moment within postmodernism, but that does so
without calling its own ontological status into question. The fragmentary

subjects, manifold ontological levels, and diffuse author functions of the Ambergris novels at first glance appear to follow experiments by writers such as Thomas Pynchon, John Barth, and Kathy Acker—experiments that not only question the world "out there" in terms of its coherence and consistency but also their own capacity to question such a world or adequately represent its incoherence and inconsistency. The Ambergris novels may aspire to such self-reflexivity, but because they do so in the service of creating a secondary world, their accomplishment in this regard cannot be considered according to techniques developed in response to texts set in and dependent on the primary world in which the reader reads. The experiments of the Ambergris novels do not reflect a world whose coherence has been undermined by late capitalism (or exposed as always already undermined, if unknowingly, before the present moment). Rather, these experiments constitute Ambergris as such. The Ambergris novels do not struggle to represent a reality "out there"; they assert a world materially conditioned by their textuality, which is part and parcel of the sort of impossibility exhibited by fantasy's secondary worlds.

The last two sections of this chapter offer a description of some of *City of Saints and Madmen*'s most prominent textual excesses and a longer examination of Duncan Shriek insofar as he emerges and disappears over the course of the Ambergris novels. The discussion of *City of Saints and Madmen*, which I compare to Mark Z. Danielewski's *House of Leaves* (2000),[16] clarifies how the Ambergris novels engage with and subvert postmodernist poetics and the world building of generic fantasy, as well as how they establish a world via a textuality that is a materiality. My discussion of Duncan Shriek's life reveals the manner in which fantastic materiality operates in the Ambergris novels and how it provides a ground for events impossible everywhere but within a world whose material condition is its textuality.

FANTASY, POSTMODERNIST POETICS, AND THE POSTTHEORY THEORY NOVEL

All of VanderMeer's major creations—the Veniss milieu, Ambergris, Area X, Borne—participate in the sort of estrangement commonly found, to different degrees and with different consequences, in the major subgenres of fantastika: fantasy, science fiction, and horror. However, Ambergris makes use of an estranging convention largely associated with fantasy, what has been called the secondary world or the otherworld. Such worlds are "autonomous worlds that are not bound to the mundane world . . . and which are impossible in terms of our normal understanding of the sciences and of history . . . and which are self-coherent in terms of Story."[17] Unlike science fiction, which demonstrates the impossibility or possibility of historical progress, and horror, which reveals the very idea of such progress to be a lie propping up a failed or failing humanity, fantasy acknowledges the reality of history even as it seeks a way out of its persistent incompleteness. Fantasy's worlds aspire to the completeness, coherence, and consistency attributed to reality beyond its representation or before representation altogether (even if reality has lost these qualities at some point as a result of some historical transformation or as a consequence of the advent of history generally).[18]

Understood in this context, Ambergris resembles the worlds of traditional fantasies, such as Tolkien's Middle-earth, C. S. Lewis's Narnia, George R. R. Martin's Westeros, and Patrick Rothfuss's Temerant. It also stands in contrast to the Veniss milieu, Area X, and the earth of *Borne*, which to one degree or another represent the reader's world—the primary world, the real earth itself, however fictionalized, futuristic, and/or unknowable these respective settings might be, however much they complicate our relationship to space and time, and however much they challenge the assumptions conditioning our thought. Ambergris only exists to the degree that texts describe and assert it as entirely the product of imagination or creation, with no claim to mimeticism or realism. Such is the case for all secondary worlds. No matter how much they borrow from the primary world—trees, the fact of social norms, a notion of cause and effect—they present to the reader places that do not exist, and often cannot exist according to assumptions about material reality likely shared by readers.[19] In order to achieve some semblance of reality, the texts describing these worlds tend to obscure their own textuality and narrativity and thus present themselves naively, less as adequate representations of something else than as truth itself.

The Lord of the Rings (1954), for example, despite constantly calling attention to the ways in which its characters take part in a long, ongoing story, never once knowingly refers to any sort of representation. All of the stories told by Gandalf, Elrond, and Galadriel are true; these characters' immortality guarantees the veracity of their accounts of even the most ancient events. In *The Two Towers*, readers encounter an example of the nonrepresentational story that would be, in its naïveté, a point of embarrassment for nearly any other sort of fiction. As Sam and Frodo complete their journey into Mordor, Sam discusses the horror experienced by Beren and Lúthien during their quest to recover the Silmaril from Morgoth: "But that's a long tale, of course, and goes past the happiness and into grief and beyond it— and the Silmaril went on and came to Eärendil. And why, sir, I never thought of that before! We've got—you've got some of the light of it in that star-glass that the Lady gave you! Why, to think of it, we're in the same tale still! It's going on. Don't the great tales never end?"[20] Sam makes clear how he and Frodo participate in the same story of good and evil that they have heard from characters such as those listed above, but neither he nor Tolkien takes this occasion to call into question the materiality of the current quest or imply its constructedness or textuality. Rather, Sam grasps all at once the meaning and coherency that his life has always possessed and that can only be achieved in an unquestioned and unquestionable story, one fundamentally bound to the world in which it takes place, and one that is the world in which it takes place.

Sam's epiphany, or rather anamnesis, is a moment of what John Clute calls recognition, which occurs when characters come to understand, or rather remember, their participation in story. "Story" in this context refers to both the structural logic or grammar of fantasy and to the true state of the world destroyed by the advent of representation and history. Reflecting on generic fantasy's desire for an Edenic existence and the language thereof, Clute writes, "Recognition marks the moment when the Story means itself." This aspect of fantasy resonates both with its structural opposition to science fiction and the nature of the worlds it creates and presents to the reader:

> In fantasy texts this recuperative, inward-turning, heart-
> lifting moment of Recognition is analogous to the moment
> of conceptual breakthrough . . . which defines the essential
> thrust outwards towards increased knowing in [science
> fiction]. Conceptual breakthrough leads through the barrier
> to a realization of what the world is; Recognition is an
> acknowledgement that one has been there all the time.[21]

If the turning point in a given science fiction narrative comes as the result of a greater understanding of the world, an understanding more true than the previous one and achieved through the sort of labor characteristic of critical thought (i.e., a cognition of what had been estranging), then fantasy's analogous moment occurs when characters come to understand how they are bound to their world by a comforting embrace that guarantees them a meaning beyond all meaning: an unproduced, essential, a priori truth. Tolkien sought such a truth, even if he understood that only god could create this truth, the world where it exists, and the relationship of subject to object in which it manifests. For Tolkien, the fantasist proved to be an adequate subcreator: "He makes a Secondary World which your mind can enter. Inside it, what he relates is 'true'; it accords with the laws of that world. You therefore believe it, while you are, as it were, inside. The moment disbelief arises, the spell is broken; the magic, or rather art, has failed."[22] Tolkien clearly understands the artificial nature of the fantasist's endeavor, but he nonetheless insists on the necessity of creating secondary or literary belief—what we might understand as the affect necessary to withstand and counteract the corrosive effects of critical–historicist thought on the modern world (which Tolkien witnessed in the trenches of World War I). In any case, the possibility of such belief depends on the subcreator's art, the ability to never call attention to the reader's act of reading, the constructedness of the secondary world in which the reader immerses herself, the textual determination of the characters she reads about, or the sophistry that grants the story its "truth."[23] Thus there are, in secondary worlds such as Middle-earth, no versions of stories, no interpretations of stories, no differences of opinion over what such stories mean. There is only the story-truth. Those who do not understand and inhabit it, or those who refuse it, have been corrupted by evil and have fallen from grace.[24]

The experiments of contemporary, postmodernist fiction stand opposed to the naive world building of genre fantasy.[25] As Brian McHale argues, postmodernist fiction privileges ontological questions above and against the epistemological questions privileged by modernist fiction without eliminating epistemological concerns altogether. McHale offers the following examples of the latter, which reflect the critical concerns of modernity: "What is there to be known?; Who knows it?; How do they know it, and with what degree of certainty?; How is knowledge transmitted from one knower to another, and with what degree of reliability?; How does the object of knowledge change as it passes from knower to knower?; What are the limits of the knowable? And so on."[26] Each of these questions challenges the human capacity to know the world and to adequately grasp reality. At the same time, the fictions that privilege these questions deprivilege other ones, and thus they tend to assume a world or materiality that might, or might not, be known. By contrast, postmodernist fiction questions the nature of the world itself and calls into doubt the coherency or consistency of the world out there beyond even the human capacity to know it. McHale writes,

> [The] typical postmodernist questions bear either on the ontology of the literary text itself or on the ontology of the world which it projects, for instance: What is a world?; What kinds of world are there, how are they constituted, and how do they differ?; What happens when different kinds of world are placed into confrontation, or when boundaries between worlds are violated?; What is the mode of existence of a text, and what is the mode of existence of the world (or worlds) it projects?; How is a projected world structured? And so on.[27]

If modernist questions skewer the naïveté allowing Sam to recognize the meaning of his life and his fundamental relationship with the history of his world, then the postmodernist ones call into question Middle-earth itself, both for Sam and for the reader. In The Lord of the Rings,

Sam's naïveté is presented as knowingness beyond knowingness, a true knowledge or anamnesis that cannot be questioned. To people like Sam, whose statements are metaphysical rather than metafictional, purveyors and fans of contemporary ironic texts can only shake their heads and note how their constructions, in contrast to Middle-earth, flatten the difference between the world in the text and the world the text is in. They grant no more reality to one or the other. For this reason, there can be communication between these two worlds—a form of communication independent of the outdated affect called belief.

Fredric Jameson's description of the opposition of pastiche to parody helps make clear the incompatibility of postmodernist fiction with genre fantasy. Pastiche, which is characteristic of postmodernism, lacks "parody's ulterior motive," and it operates "without the satirical impulse, without laughter, without that still latent feeling that there exists something normal compared to which what is being imitated is rather comic."[28] Similarly, postmodernist fiction is critical but denies any norm against which its criticality can be judged. It therefore lacks the historicist drive to progress, and it thus cuts things down without a project for producing something else. Generic fantasy cannot survive such acid, which dissolves our capacity to interact with what does not conform to a given notion of the real—a real that cannot be represented but that must be assumed as a norm, in the material sense, nonetheless.[29]

Timothy Clarke and other thinkers of the Anthropocene would remind us how our very capacity to ask these questions, even questions calling into question the world or the text conveying a narrative, assumes the material earth as its condition. Clarke does not ask the postmodernist skeptic to "go kick a rock" if she questions the reality of her world, but rather he reminds us that even such skepticism derives from humanist assumptions produced by certain types of delimitation. We can think about *this*, or think in general, because we do not (or cannot) think about *that* at the same time. To put all of this another way, the problem with the sorts of questions McHale lists, from the point of view of new weird fiction and cultural geology, is the very possibility of questioning, which must assume a materiality that makes questioning possible, whatever this materiality's characteristics as a world. Karl Rove's famous statement about a reality-based community whose time has passed, and the Trump administration's clamoring about fake news and alternative facts even as it destroys the prospect of political communication with its daily mendacity and obfuscation, reveal the extent to which certain forms of skepticism are corrosive to society. Yet a return to the sort of belief Tolkien values seems impossible, given how historical "progress" has produced our current state of affairs.

The Ambergris novels—especially *City of Saints and Madmen*, with its multiple recursive, fragmentary narratives and excessive design, and *Shriek: An Afterword*, with its metafictional devices and absent authors—seem at first glance to take this skepticism and use it to skewer the naïveté exhibited by Tolkien and Sam. However, Ambergris's status as a secondary world or otherworld challenges this assumption even as VanderMeer's postmodernist poetics render any unalloyed belief in Ambergris impossible. The juxtaposition of the world building of generic fantasy with the experiments in form and media associated with postmodernist fiction proves startling. VanderMeer addresses this very issue: "I found that using these techniques to support fiction set in a fantastical city changed the context of the postmodern technique considerably. Which is to say, those techniques that might be said to break the fourth wall instead reinforced the reality of the fantasy."[30] It is the nature of this reality—or, better, this materiality—of fantasy that I aim to investigate here. Far from privileging questions of ontology over questions of epistemology (or questions of epistemology over questions of ontology), the Ambergris novels undo the question of questions altogether. Ambergris undermines the humanist assumption that questions can be asked and answered, even when this assumption acknowledges the necessarily imperfect or intentionally misleading nature of answers. Any question must presuppose a materiality conditioning a subject who asks the question. The Ambergris novels produce their own form of materiality, one bound up with textuality and nonetheless defying the bottomless pit of postmodernist poetics. If fantasy seeks to create a story that means itself, and if postmodernist poetics suggest that textuality can only ever collapse on itself to the point where all potential for meaning is liquidated, then the Ambergris novels deploy a textuality that is itself—a textuality that is the material condition of a world.

Mitchum Huehls's theorization of what he calls the posttheory theory novel suggests the intersection of world building and postmodernist poetics found in the Ambergris novels is not unique (although VanderMeer's generic commitments render these novels peculiar examples of the form). For Huehls, posttheory theory novels are "those contemporary works of fiction written in the wake of theory's decline, that use well-known theoretical concepts—for example, the death of the author, the materiality of the signifier, the textuality of the world, the recursivity of the reference—without reflexively applying these concepts to the text itself."[31] Huehls offers both a rough taxonomy of posttheory theory novels and instances of these types. Jeffrey Eugenides's *The Marriage Plot* (2011), for example, exhibits strong realist tendencies in the wake of theory in order to "describe and deploy theory as a symptomatic historical phenomenon."[32] As worthy as this goal is, Huehls finds other instances of the posttheory theory novel more interesting and important—instances bearing on the Ambergris novels' dual engagement with the worlds of generic fantasy and the textuality of postmodernist fiction:

> These novels treat theory's concepts in a way that's almost perfectly opposed to how theory novels of old engaged those same concepts. For example, rather than emphasizing the word's inevitable mediation of the world—a mediation that in theory novels indicates our insuperable alienation from the real—post-theory theory novels incorporate the word into the world, using language to build new, idiosyncratic notions of the real. Consistently declining theory's invitation to turn their conditions of possibility against themselves, these texts use theory's concepts to build, rather than undermine, the world. They speak the language of theory without necessarily giving themselves over to it.[33]

Under the condition of the Anthropocene, any assumption or assertion of humanity's "insuperable alienation from the real" will come across as denial or cynicism at best and malpractice at worst. As such, producers of fictions have struggled to represent, express, or designate the temporal and spatial scales at which geologic forces work as well as the manner in which humanity interacts with these scales and forces. Likewise, critics and scholars have sought to develop vocabulary and concepts that allow them to discuss literary forms and modes so engaged without reducing them to the endless recursion of an inescapable textuality or representation.[34] Bruno Latour's conceptualization of fiction as the mode of existence called [FIC], discussed in chapter 1, exemplifies the sort of thinking necessary at the present moment and demonstrates the material force literary texts can muster when we understand them as more than the mere textuality suggested by postmodernist fiction and by simplistic readings of poststructuralist theory.

Although Huehls does not explicitly concern himself with the Anthropocene in his discussion of the posttheory theory novel, he nonetheless makes clear that the relationship between word and world, and between text and materiality, does not reduce to what are commonly understood as merely literary devices such as metaphor. As he puts it elsewhere, "The representational logic of metaphor doesn't work anymore. Suggesting that one thing stands in for, points to, refers to, allegorizes, represents, portrays, or signifies some other thing no longer yields productive or actionable meaning."[35] Fantasy has long recognized the importance of the nonallegorical, a recognition allowing for the sort of world building it so often undertakes. Tolkien himself dismissed claims about how The Lord of the Rings allegorizes World War II.[36] E. R. Eddison, in the dedication to a 1922 protofantasy much admired by Tolkien, writes, "It is neither allegory nor fable but a Story to be read for its own sake."[37] Stephen R. Donaldson makes similar claims about the nonallegorical in fantasy.[38]

Not surprisingly, the naïveté fantasy expresses through its attempts to mean only itself, to turn inward and away from meaning conventionally understood as representation, is at the root of condemnations of it. For historical materialists, because fantasy does not adequately represent the real world and the labor out of which its history is made, it must be understood as a shallow symptom of capitalist ideology. Carl Freedman, for example, dismisses Middle-earth as being "miles wide but only inches deep. Frequently celebrated for all it contains— the various species, the colourful names, the invented languages, the intricate geography, and so forth—it is even more noteworthy for what it lacks. . . . Middle-earth leaves out most of what makes us real human beings living in a real historical society."[39] Given the urgency of the material situation presented by the Anthropocene, liquidating our literature of what makes us human—namely the assumptions about history and critical thought that have in part led to the Anthropocene—might be worth considering. The Ambergris novels, taken together, offer a peculiar and powerful example of the posttheory theory novel. These are novels that begin in what appears to be a pure textuality from which there is no way out and end with a nascent materiality built of this textuality. They refuse to flatten the distinction between world and word by asserting everything is text. Instead, they tell us "there may be a way," then demonstrate how everything is material. As such, these novels embody the capacity of literary texts not only to represent a given world assumed by anthropocentric and anthropomorphic thought but also to intervene in and create this world.

"THIS *IS* AMBERGRIS": THE TEXTUAL WORLD OF *CITY OF SAINTS AND MADMEN*

Like so many postmodernist fictions, *City of Saints and Madmen* revels in its textuality and denies the coherency often attributed to the novel in its realist mode—which still remains, for some cultural critics and much of the reading public, the novel's implicitly proper form. That we can call it a novel at all surely tells us something about the expansion the term enjoyed in the wake of the formal and textual experiments of the twentieth century starting with Joyce, Stein, and Proust and continuing through and beyond Burroughs, Reed, Pynchon, and Acker (among numerous others). However, *City of Saints and Madmen* also initiates a world-building exercise, and it is the interaction of a secondary world apposite generic fantasy with a postmodernist poetics reminiscent of the most excessive experiments of the postwar period that grants the novel its uniqueness and power. I shall turn below to the nature of the Ambergris novels' world building, and how it depends on the textuality inaugurated in *City of Saints and Madmen*. For now, a brief description of the first Ambergris novel and some of its textual features will allow me to compare it to another exemplary text of late postmodernist fiction, Mark Z. Danielewski's *House of Leaves* (2000), and thus make clear how its engagement with generic fantasy overcomes the textual abyss Janice Shriek seems to fear. If the climactic moment of fantasy reveals a story that means itself through a refusal of representation, then *City of Saints and Madmen* begins to demonstrate how Ambergris grounds itself as world on a materiality consisting of textuality.

City of Saints and Madmen comprises two parts: "The Book of Ambergris," which is itself divided into four novella-length texts of various types, and an Appendix, which purports to consist of texts found in the possession of a character in the final section of "The Book of Ambergris." Examples of the extremity of *City of Saints and Madmen*'s textual condition, which in no way constitute a comprehensive list, include the following:

> *Dradin, in Love*, the first section of "The Book of Ambergris,"
> at first seems to be a straightforward narrative about a
> missionary, Dradin, returning to Ambergris from abroad,
> set in a secondary world and produced by a writer named Jeff
> VanderMeer.[40] However, in "The Strange Case of X," the final
> part of "The Book of Ambergris," a writer named X claims to
> have written the three texts the reader has just read, including
> *Dradin, in Love*. Still later in *City of Saints and Madmen*,
> *Dradin, in Love* turns out to be a text published in Ambergris,
> one written by Dradin himself. Frederick Madnok's *King
> Squid*, one text among those found in the Appendix, cites
> "Dradin Kashmir's third-person autobiography, *Dradin, in
> Love*" as a dubious source of information on the Festival of
> the Freshwater Squid.[41] In *Shriek: An Afterword*, *Dradin, in*

Love appears as the subject of one of Mary Sabon's academic monographs: *The Gray Caps' Role in Modern Literature: The Dilemma of Dradin, in Love*. In short, *Dradin, in Love* at first appears to be a fairly conventional, if grim and at times surrealistic, secondary world fantasy. Upon further examination, however, its status as a story and the status of the world this story represents are called into question along the lines McHale describes. *Dradin, in Love* begins the process by which the materiality of Ambergris and the textuality of the Ambergris novels are revealed to be one and the same thing. Like many of the texts found in the several versions of *City of Saints and Madmen*, *Dradin, in Love* appeared before the novel's publication as a stand-alone trade paperback in 1996.

"The Strange Case of X," the fourth and final section in "The Book of Ambergris," reveals each of the three texts which precede it—*Dradin, in Love*, *The Hoegbotton Guide to the Early History of Ambergris*, and *The Transformation of Martin Lake*—to exist within *City of Saints and Madmen*, written by a writer named X, who claims to be from Chicago. X, one of at least two VanderMeer analogs in the series (Duncan Shriek being the other[42]) insists he has invented Ambergris and everything in it. Nonetheless, he also insists to an unnamed examiner in a strange psychiatric hospital that Ambergris is real and that he has been there. Additionally, X confesses to having murdered a woman named Janice Shriek, who once gave him a book called *The Hoegbotton Guide to the Early History of Ambergris* as a birthday gift. Janice had claimed to have purchased the book in Borges Bookstore on Ambergris's interminable Albumuth Boulevard. X further claims to have visited Ambergris on several occasions, through unknown means. Throughout the story, X assumes his interrogator, a fellow American and Chicagoan, not to believe him about the murder or his travels. Indeed, by the story's conclusion, the examiner makes clear he does not believe X, but for a reason different than what X expects. In his final words to X, the examiners states, "This *is* Ambergris. You are *in* Ambergris."[43] Just as *Dradin, in Love* becomes a point of intersection between the world building of fantasy and postmodernist poetics and thereby an example of a peculiar relationship between materiality and textuality, this statement acknowledges how those in Ambergris stand on a materiality consisting of textuality.

The Appendix that follows "The Book of Ambergris" comprises mainly texts found among X's things by the examiner from "The Strange Case of X." Two are written by this examiner in an attempt to catalog and describe these texts to someone else and to account for his attempts at deciphering them. They include several fictions by writers from Ambergris; a pseudo-scientific, para-academic account of the Ambergrisian freshwater squid, rendered dubious by its writer's strange attraction to the squid and his desire to become one (complete with an extensively annotated bibliography of fake works in which the writer's predilections are revealed); a glossary of Ambergrisian vocabulary, the provenance of which is unknown; a family history of one of Ambergris's powerful merchant houses; and an encrypted text.

This last text, entitled "The Man Who Had No Eyes" in the final paperback edition of *City of Saints and Madmen*, is especially interesting. It consists of fifteen "paragraphs," each comprising several punctuated "sentences." The "words" forming each sentence are strings of four numerals (e.g., 13:1:5:1, 64:5:1:3). These numerals, respectively, refer to a page number, paragraph number, line number, and word number from "The Book of Ambergris" and the foreword to *City of Saints and Madmen* by Michael Moorcock. The process of decrypting the text proves startling insofar as the reader will discover words in contexts that ramify with the themes of the story being decrypted, as with the third word of the first paragraph, "a." This article is located in the first paragraph in *Dradin, in Love,* where it precedes "machine." In its new context, it echoes the Machine built by the gray caps to help them return to their home beyond Ambergris—a machine Duncan Shriek has discovered by the time he writes the *Guide,* and one that plays a major role in *Finch* (to which "The Man Who Had No Eyes" provides a prequel of sorts insofar as it narrates events directly leading to the situation with which *Finch* begins). The sixteenth paragraph of the story is similarly composed, but the strings making up each word are only two numerals long (e.g., 1:1, 15:4). The numerals in these strings refer, respectively, to the first fifteen paragraphs in "The Man Who Had No Eyes" and the words that make up these paragraphs. In the final paperback edition of *Saints,* the first fifteen paragraphs of the story have been decrypted by the person who finds it, X's examiner. In a letter preceding the decryption, he notes he cannot figure out the last section (likely because of its recursivity). The reader must decrypt it for herself. In the hardcover edition, the full text needs to be decrypted.[44]

Beyond all of this, the novel's graphic dimensions contribute to its textuality. Frontispieces from the Ambergris editions of the four parts of "The Book of Ambergris" introduce each of those texts. The typefaces in the Appendix change from text to text, implying their "original" publication venues. (VanderMeer provides fictional histories for these typefaces after the Appendix. Similarly, he provides a partially fictional list of publications for himself before the beginning of the novel.) Along similar lines, the pagination of the Appendix does not follow from the pagination of "The Book of Ambergris," which is continuous despite the four separate narratives and specific publication histories of the texts it consists of. Rather, the several parts of the Appendix follow paginations specific to their Ambergrisian venues of publication, or they eschew pagination altogether if their original forms warrant (as in the case of letters, for example). The dust jacket to the hardcover edition of the novel features a story not found in the paperback edition. Additionally, VanderMeer implies in numerous places that many of the texts in the Appendix were not originally conceived as part of Ambergris.[45]

Each of these elements is worth greater consideration, although space and a desire for clarity prevent me from further analysis of them here. Suffice it to say that *City of Saints and Madmen*, to a degree that would make many other postmodern encyclopedic novels blush, presents itself as a text incapable of containing itself and as a novel that questions its capacity to be a novel or to represent something outside of itself. In contrast to other such novels, however, it endeavors to avoid even a critique of representation. It eschews the question of representation altogether, along with all of the critical baggage associated with this question. By turning inward—toward itself as a world created rather than one represented—it produces a textuality coextensive with materiality, a fantastic materiality only to be found in the pages of a book. *City of Saints and Madmen* refuses to fall into the trap presented by mimetic fiction, one often taken up by science fiction and (negatively) by postmodernist fiction and horror. These forms either assume a world out there, a materiality by which they might measure their own truthfulness, or seek to demonstrate the impossibility of anthropocentric techniques' capacities to reflect or produce a truth so measured and measurable. By contrast, *City of Saints and Madmen* produces a world within itself conditioned by a materiality of textuality, an extension of itself within itself, without any regard to external conditions. What is possible in Ambergris, we discover, is what is possible within a text, and nowhere else. In Ambergris, the affordances of textuality define the limits of a fantastic materiality.

A comparison with a specific, highly apposite, and roughly contemporaneous fiction of late postmodernism will help to clarify some of these points. VanderMeer had not yet read *House of Leaves* when he initially created Ambergris.[46] Nonetheless, Ambergris, as a materiality consisting of its textuality, afforded VanderMeer the opportunity to make use of and extend Mark Z. Danielewski's experiments when it came time to design the hardcover edition.[47] The formal and textual experiments of Danielewski's novel, where endless layers of mediation allow the text to bleed into the world and force the reader to question her own reality, intriguingly resonate with those found in *City of Saints and Madmen*, although they are greatly transformed in their new context, as I shall discuss.

House of Leaves forces readers to move beyond simple assumptions about literary fiction and the realism to which it often remains implicitly bound. For example, *House of Leaves* refers to nonexistent editions of itself on its copyright page. These references enjoin the novel's narrative to overflow the material pages supposedly containing it and infect the world in which the reader reads. *City of Saints and Madmen* similarly blurs the line between word and world. VanderMeer explains: "The conceit behind the book is not to wink or blink—in other words, except in the acknowledgements, make the whole book an artifact, make every element of the book, even the list of books in the front and the font notes at the back, part of the story."[48] This textual conceit, insofar as it creates a world, provides an interesting example of the story that "means itself" and reveals an effect rather different than the one produced by *House of Leaves*: the materialization, or worlding, of the text rather than the textualization of the material. Consider N. Katherine Hayles's argument about *House of Leaves*. For Hayles, Danielewski's novel

> instantiates the crisis characteristic of postmodernism, in which representation is short-circuited by the realization that there is no reality independent of mediation. The book does not try to penetrate through cultural constructions to reach an original object of inquiry—an impossible task. On the contrary, it uses the very multi-layered inscriptions that create the book as a physical artifact to imagine the subject as a palimpsest, emerging not behind but through the inscriptions that bring the book into being.[49]

Critics such as Hayles and Mark B. N. Hansen demonstrate how *House of Leaves* helps to recuperate the novel for an historical moment without a need for printed books. However, it does so by extending certain devices of postmodernist fiction in concert with the remediation characteristic of the digital age in order to create an endlessly layered account of materiality which draws the real world into itself and finally has no bottom.[50] Danielewski constructs an object in which mysterious, invisible editors edit Johnny Truant, who edits Zampanò's notes, which describe a nonexistent film, about which there is a body of impossible scholarship no one has read—and so on. Such a bottomless pit of textuality does not adequately address the material condition called the Anthropocene.

In the textuality of *House of Leaves*, we find a criticality run amok. This criticality allows for no foundation or ground and is characteristic of genre horror. In fact, *House of Leaves*'s ruminations about contemporary media reflect and update one of horror's long-standing concerns. For example, in *Dracula* (1897), Jonathan Harker laments the inadequacy of media for capturing the supernatural, what falls outside of normal experience and knowledge: "I took the papers from the safe where they had been ever since our return so long ago. We were struck with the fact, that in all the mass of material of which the record is composed, there is hardly one authentic document; nothing but a mass of typewriting, except the later note-books of Mina and Seward and myself, and Van Helsing's memorandum. We could hardly ask any one, even did we wish to, to accept these as proofs of so wild a story."[51] *House of Leaves* similarly demonstrates the limits of anthropocentric and anthropomorphic representational systems. These limits remain in place despite the progress such systems have made in an era determined by computation and connectivity. Danielewski composed his novel in the world of the late twentieth century, a world increasingly defined by technologies that seemed to offer a way out of history as well as an end to temporal and spatial limits of human knowledge practices by way of the lossless archiving of bits and their instantaneous transmission through space. Nonetheless, the novel's events and characters fall into what Janice Shriek would call the "space between each word." Because *House of Leaves* is first and foremost a horror novel, this space—comprising layers of text, authorship, and media without end—takes the form of an abyss. The various media with which *House of Leaves* involves itself come to seem less a part of materiality than what reveals the material to be fungible.

By contrast, the events and characters of *City of Saints and Madmen*, a novel engaged with the naïveté of fantasy rather than the criticality of horror (which is a nihilistic acceleration *cum* transformation of the criticality found in science fiction), "fall" into a "space" that is itself the "bottom." The materiality of Ambergris consists of this textual space because *City of Saints and Madmen* does not initiate the representation of a world but rather the instantiation of one. As a result of this instantiation, the Ambergris novels do not involve themselves with an unacknowledged materiality, and they do not rely on any outside by which to measure the veracity or usefulness of their fictions. Rather, they assert the materiality of that which is conditioned by itself. They are not engaged with cognitive estrangement or science fiction, terms that designate and describe horror fictions that arrive at happier endings. All such fictions seek a representation adequate to some anthropomorphic notion of truth. *City of Saints and Madmen* engages with a fantastic materiality whose truth derives from its own creation through the sort of textuality formerly deployed against such materiality. Whereas realist fiction, in a manner similar to science fiction, assumes the presence of a materiality out there against which fictions can be measured, and whereas *House of Leaves* seeks to (yet again) undermine the possibility of such measurement and the commensurability it implies and assumes, *City of Saints and Madmen* seeks to produce, or fantasize, its own materialism. It accomplishes this endeavor through its excessive textuality, which occupies the space created by the indefinite pronoun in one of the novel's most important lines: "This *is* Ambergris."

"I WAS *BECOMING* IT": THE TEXTUAL AND MATERIAL LIVES OF DUNCAN SHRIEK

Those who read the Ambergris novels in the order in which they were published, and who read each beginning with its first page and proceeding to its last, will initially encounter Duncan Shriek as the writer of

The Hoegbotton Guide to the Early History of Ambergris, the second section of "The Book of Ambergris" in *City of Saints and Madmen.*[52] Such readers—lacking any context or backstory for the *Guide* or its writer, or any knowledge of the conflicts with which each is involved—will likely think very little of Duncan. He presents himself, to the extent he presents himself at all, as a bit of a crank: someone with perhaps a personal ax to grind about the matters he discusses and the people to whom he addresses this discussion, but finally someone of little obvious consequence. By the time such readers finish *Shriek: An Afterword,* they will have discovered how Duncan's personal life, specifically his involvement with his student, Mary Sabon, as well as his scholarship, deemed unorthodox at best and dangerous at worst, have led him to a situation where the only work he can get is writing a guide meant for tourists, published by a mercantile family with little interest in anything but profit. This guide, it turns out, embodies Duncan's last attempt to communicate to the public his theories about the gray caps and their role in the history of Ambergris.

Unfortunately, this attempt will fail. The editors and Hoegbotton & Sons deem the manuscript of the *Guide* too long and too unorthodox for its intended audience. In Duncan's absence, and in light of his apparent unwillingness to write in a manner fit for public consumption, the task of editing the manuscript into something acceptable falls on Janice, for whom it provides an opportunity to write an afterword describing Duncan's life. As she contemplates her nearly finished task, Janice wonders why Duncan has never taken a stronger stand for his positions and why he has never fought harder to convince people of his theories about the history and nature of Ambergris, all of which have been disputed and discredited by Mary Sabon and the city's intelligentsia. Duncan responds to Janice in the only way he can to someone still thinking according to representationalist, textualist logic: paratextually, parenthetically, as something apart from the text that nonetheless expresses itself in text. "{Because, Janice, I was *becoming* what I believed in. I was *becoming* it. And it might have been strange and unknown, never to be recognized, but it meant more to me than words on a page by then.}"[53]

What concerns me here is the nature of this becoming, which exemplifies the fantastic materiality inaugurated in *City of Saints and Madmen* and developed in *Shriek: An Afterword* and *Finch*. To grasp the nature of this becoming, we must first understand the nature of Duncan's existence in the novels, obscured as it is by our own textualist assumptions and characterized by constant appearances and disappearances. To readers bound to the logic of representation by which texts imperfectly refer to and gesture toward things outside of themselves, and to readers who understand that the spaces between words consist of bottomless pits where any possibility of reaching the material world disappears, Duncan's appearances and disappearances will seem to signify his subordination to textuality produced by others, a textuality of which "we're told, from birth until our deathbed, in a thousand spoken and unspoken ways" no one makes it out. However, when Ambergris is grasped as a whole—not as a rectilinear narrative unfolding in time but as a complete materiality bound together by what Duncan Shriek becomes—we see how there may be a way.

If we assume for the moment that Duncan remains subordinate to a pervasive textuality as the writer of *The Hoegbotton Guide to the Early History of Ambergris*—which constrains him by way of its circumstances of publication, its editing at the hands of his sister, its limited capacity to represent a specialized argument, and its audience—then his disappearance from the *Guide*, which he announces in a late footnote, implies the sort of falling into the spaces between the words Janice fears. If taken as such, it implies a final loss of subjectivity, autonomy, and agency. Indeed, over the next two sections of "The Book of Ambergris," and throughout the entirety of the Appendix, Duncan only appears as a name spoken or written by others, one attached to texts among other texts or one designating an historian among other historians, someone of no lasting importance. Although he is the titular character (or one of the titular characters) of the second Ambergris novel, he seems to fare little better in *Shriek*. There he appears first as the subject of Mary Sabon's insult, second as the subject of his sister's representation, and third as parenthetical/paratextual responses to this representation. If his footnotes to the *Guide* allow him some capacity to insert himself into Ambergris as an autonomous agent, then this capacity seems diminished in *Shriek* to the extent that he can only react to a text produced by someone else.

However, any diminishments of subjectivity, agency, or autonomy Duncan suffers only manifest as epiphenomena to his attempts to communicate with those who remain trapped in representationalist and textualist logic—and the forms of subjectivity dependent on such logic. By the time he disappears in *The Hoegbotton Guide to the Early History of Ambergris*, an event described from Janice's uncomprehending point of view in the final pages of *Shriek*, Duncan is in the process of becoming something that retains its humanity only for the purpose of speaking to humans. His new form, his way out, allows him to escape the logics under which such communication normally takes place. In *Finch*— which largely eschews the textuality of *City and Saints and Madmen* and *Shriek* in order to present a world unwritten by any of the characters in it but rather materially determined by Duncan himself—he concludes this transformation. There he appears first as a memory experienced by the detective after whom the book is named, then as a material being consisting of this detective's flesh. In his final form, he is no longer described by any writer other than the one whose name appears on the novel's cover (i.e., "Jeff VanderMeer"). He is no longer textualized by other beings or forms who remain utterly bound to a purely textual condition. Rather, he reveals himself to have escaped from this subordination at a much earlier date, but in a manner he cannot communicate through conventional, textualist means. Duncan, in the end (and at the beginning, because his becoming involves the liquidation of such markers), reveals the limitations under which the people of Ambergris, who believe they inhabit a world in need of representing rather than one in need of shaping, operate and allows those who disappeared during the Silence to return and begin a rebellion against the gray caps, whose materiality has infiltrated every aspect of Ambergrisian life. In coming to understand the gray caps and the role they have played in Ambergris since the time of the city's founding, Duncan grasps the possibilities inherent to fantastic materiality.

I shall turn to these possibilities momentarily. For now, I shall stay with the *Guide* to provide some background on the history of Ambergris in order to further elaborate on Duncan's unorthodox views on this history and to describe the reasoning behind his withdrawal from this history at the conclusion to the *Guide*. Briefly, the history of Ambergris, according to the *Guide*, involves the arrival of a whaler *cum* pirate, Cappan John Manzikert, on the shores of the River Moth; Manzikert's subsequent slaughter of the gray caps already living at this location; the disappearance of Manzikert and the Truffidian monk, Samuel Tonsure, into the fungal underworld below the fledgling city; the reappearance of Manizkert, minus his eyes; the even later reappearance of Tonsure's journal (along with the aforementioned eyes); and the holocaust known as the Silence, during which nearly the entire population of Ambergris disappeared. The final section of the *Guide* ruminates about Tonsure's journal and its missing final page. Regardless of the impression this history makes as a matter of fact on its readers, these readers will likely not be able to fully appreciate Duncan's tone, which, especially in the context of the events of *Shriek* and *Finch*, reveals itself to be skeptical of official history, hostile to Manzikert, and willing to question the nature of reality itself (especially with regard to Ambergris's utter lack of anything like a civil government or institutions of power beyond universities and art galleries). Moreover, the personal dimension of Duncan's commentary will fail to impress itself on readers new to Ambergris as anything but the animosity of a spurned lover. Clearly something has taken place between Duncan and someone known as Mary Sabon, but the *Guide* does not reveal how the conflict between them reflects a larger conflict about the nature of Ambergris itself. Something has caused Duncan to write this pamphlet, meant for a popular rather than expert audience, rather than the scholarship he formerly produced, but the nature of Duncan's fall only seems, insofar as the *Guide* can describe, to be a function of his resolute iconoclasm, an inability to play nicely with others.

To take but one important example of the way in which a reader new to Ambergris might misunderstand Duncan as he appears in the *Guide*, consider his discussion of the Silence. He begins this discussion with, "An historian must take extreme care when discussing the Silence, for the enormity of the event demands respect."[54] During the Silence, which took place several centuries before the events described in *Shriek: An*

Afterword, 25,000 people—nearly the entire population of Ambergris—disappeared, seemingly in midmeal, without any warning and without any sign of struggle. (The only ones who did not disappear were away from the city at the time.) As numerous scholars of the Shoah make clear, and as Duncan seems to be saying, one must approach death at a certain scale, and death without any rational reason behind it, with a certain reverence and with a great deal of care. However, it becomes clear in *Shriek* that at best Duncan is being ironic. The Silence, he argues, was not an attack by the gray caps but rather a mistake made by beings who not only do not care about humans but also think in ways altogether exclusive of human notions of caring. During an argument about this topic summarized by Janice, Duncan exclaims, "Would it be easier to accept that they don't give a damn about us one way or the other if we hadn't massacred them to build this city? What I think is crazy is that we try to pretend that they are just like us. If we had massacred most of the citizens of Morrow, we would expect them to seek revenge. That would be natural, understandable, even acceptable. But what about a people that, when you slaughter hundreds of them, doesn't even really notice?"[55]

Janice is infuriated by the suggestion that the Silence might be something other than the official story about it: a hostile action granting the citizens of Ambergris a certain importance, a role in an ongoing struggle for recognition or resources with an other that simply reflects the self in opposite terms. More important than Janice's reaction, or even Duncan's specific arguments about the Silence and the gray caps revealed here, is what this conversation reveals about the respect Duncan invokes in the *Guide,* a respect he clearly feigns so as to not ruffle feathers among the people of Ambergris or within the field of Ambergrisian history—or one imposed on Duncan by Janice, who cannot follow her brother in this line of thinking. Whatever the case, Duncan does not respect the Silence as a holocaust because he does not understand it to be one. Indeed, in the final pages of *Finch,* many of its victims turn out to be alive. As revealed in *Shriek* and *Finch,* the Silence is a mistake made in the writing of a world whose materiality and textuality are, for those with the capacities to properly see this oneness, one and the same thing. Janice's reaction to Duncan's claim can then be read as the reaction of someone for whom proper representation is part and parcel of being a proper human being. Duncan's statement thus becomes an ironic one, indicating his contempt for official history, but only as his story is slowly revealed in subsequent texts and only after he frees himself finally from the need to exist in the textual condition in which he finds himself in *City of Saints and Madmen*.

Duncan's self-liberation comes with his disappearance from the *Guide*, the process for which he commences at the start of its final section, after he concludes his discussion of the Silence and before he begins to ruminate on the nature of the journal of Samuel Tonsure. In the 108th footnote to the *Guide*, a footnote appended to the "IV" with which this section of the *Guide* starts, Duncan writes:

> At this point in the narrative I begin to make my *formal*
> farewells, for those of you who ever even noticed my *marginal*
> existence. By now *the blind mechanism of the story* has surpassed
> me, and I shall jump out of the way in order to let it roll on,
> unimpeded by my frantic gesticulations for attention. The
> *time-bound* history is done: there is only the matter of sweeping
> the floors, taking out the garbage, and turning off the lights.
> Meanwhile, I shall retire once more to the anonymity of my
> little apartment overlooking the Voss Bender Memorial Square.
> This is the fate of historians: to fade ever more into the fabric
> of their history, until they finally no longer exist outside of it.
> Remember this while you navigate the afternoon crowd in the
> Religious Quarter, your guidebook held limply in your pudgy
> left hand as your right struggles to balance a half-pint of bitter.[56]

There is much in this paragraph worth considering, primarily the contempt it directs at the reader, wandering about Ambergris with nothing but writing as a guide, drinking despite the pervasive danger that exists, invisible to those bound by textuality and representation. Duncan here takes "formal" farewells from a "marginal" existence—the sort of existence one has in a text that is merely text. This farewell thus suggests another existence characterized by greater materiality. Duncan knows that the "blind mechanism of story," part of the blindness Mary Sabon once had stripped from her by Duncan's glasses, overcomes any attempt to communicate about materiality to those who are constitutively unable to understand it. His disposal of "time-bound" history suggests an escape from the rectilinearity of historical narrative and an escape from the proper chain of cause and effect. Indeed, in *Finch*, he will reveal himself to be not only capable of self-resurrection but also able to move about within and beyond the Ambergris texts at will, no longer subordinated to these texts qua textuality, no longer fearful of the abyss Janice fears, and no longer conditioned by a given materiality out there that a text might at best seek to represent or undermine. By the time he appears in *Finch*, he will have become a master of a fantastic materiality—a materiality that is textuality.

This movement is facilitated by a becoming-fungal that allows Duncan to spread throughout Ambergris invisibly even while his fruiting body visibly manifests here and there as necessary. Fruiting bodies are the most visible part of the fungi; most people associate them with mushrooms. Mushrooms are in fact these fruiting bodies, and they signify a much larger, and more diffuse, organism inhabiting whatever substrate the mushroom grows on. This larger part of the fungus, called the mycelium, inveigles its way into that substrate by way of tendril-like hyphae, which branch throughout soil, wood, and so on. Through means never fully explained, but hinted to involve prolonged exposure to the world of the gray caps and their technologies, Duncan's body becomes fungal and manifests fruiting bodies on its surface. As Janice helps Duncan remove a dying layer of his new form, she describes it as follows:

> A madness of mushrooms, mottling his skin—no uniform
> shape of variety or size. Some pulsed a strobing pink-blue.
> Others radiates a dull, deep burgundy. A few hung from his
> waist like upside-down wineglasses, translucent and hollow,
> the space inside filled with clusters of tiny button-shaped
> green-gold nodules that disintegrated at the slightest touch.
> Textures from rough to smooth rippled to grainy to slick.

Smells—the smells all ran together into an earthy but not
unpleasant tang, punctuated by a hint of mint.[57]

Duncan revels in his new state of being. He explains how it cannot be
reduced to what is visible to others: "I was magnificent. Every part of
my body was *receiving*. I could 'hear' things through my body, feel them,
that no human short of Samuel Tonsure could understand."[58] Duncan
not only looks different but also exists differently; he exists according to
affects human beings cannot grasp and is attuned to stimuli beyond the
human sensorium. His visible body suggests a much larger entity existing in a substrate. This substrate, of course, is Ambergris itself—insofar
as Ambergris is a material text that conditions a world. By becoming
fungal, Duncan infiltrates and fills the spaces between the words, spaces
no one else has thought to navigate for fear of falling into the abyss
Janice intuits there. Duncan demonstrates that, contrary to what Sabon
assumes and what even Janice fears, these spaces are the stuff of materiality itself when textuality is given free rein to create.

The resonance of Duncan's transformation with two machines, each
associated with writing, reveals its significance. First, consider the typewriter Janice uses to compose her afterword—a typewriter colonized by
the sort of fungus that is crucial to Duncan's becoming. As she writes,
this fungus frequently impedes her work: "I had to stop to clean off the
typewriter keys. The green fungus had become too insidious."[59] After
Janice disappears from the text, the editor of the *Guide* discovers the
typewriter, which he photographs.[60] By then, it has nearly completed its
decomposition: "The typewriter had become clogged with a green lichen
or fungus; the entire shell overtaken by the spread of this loamy green
substance."[61] That the spaces between the keys have been colonized by
fungus suggests Duncan's power to not only move throughout extant
texts and affect them in a material fashion but also to create such texts
and bind them together by way of his transformation. This is a power
Duncan seems to discover through and acquire in his encounter with
another machine: the machine the gray caps have built below Ambergris
as a means by which to return to their home on another world, a machine
whose malfunction caused the victims of the Silence to be transported

to other worlds, and a machine Duncan explicitly compares to a book: "There is no history, no present. There are only the sides of the machine. Slick memory of metal, mad with its own brightness, mad with the memory of what it contains. You cling to those sides for support, but make your way past them as quickly as possible. The sides are like the middle of a book—necessary, but quickly read through to get to the end. Already, you try in vain to forget the beginning."[62] The machine reveals past and present, beginnings and ends, to be human constructions; they are the sort of limitations that setting involves. None of these limitations exists except insofar as humans demand them for the purpose of making their lives mean something beyond the brute materiality conditioning them. They are the tools and by-products of narratives the subsequent critique of which inevitability reveals such limitations as limitations and that reveals their inadequacy with regard to the materiality out there they purport to represent. Janice's typewriter and the gray caps' machine avoid this problem of representation by treating textuality and materiality as the same thing; they treat interstices, the spaces between words, as materiality itself, albeit a fantastic materiality amenable to editing and transformation.

Duncan's disappearances from the *Guide* in *City and Saints and Madmen* and from *Shriek: An Afterword* (which are the same disappearance, narrated in two different ways) are thus less sinister than they might otherwise appear. He does not become trapped in the Ambergrisian text; rather, he enters this text and uses it as a substrate through which his tendrils might move. He can thus appear anywhere within this text, free from his subordination to the causal chains of history and narrative, free from past and present, free from beginnings and endings. He describes the sensation of this freedom, which he finds during one of his own forays into the gray caps' underground world: "That is one thing I prefer about the underground: the loss of self to your environment is almost as profound as orgasm or epiphany, your senses shattered, rippled, as fragmented and wide as the sky. Time releases its meaning. Space is just a subset of time. You cease to become mortal." Thus, the underground allows him to "lose himself without being lost" and is akin to becoming "as still as death but not dead."[63] Duncan's description of his manner of world inhabitation after his becoming sheds light onto a passage from his journal that Janice clearly misunderstands: "Should the historian's personal life happen to coincide in some way with the history he has chosen to write about—if the personal history 'doubles' the public history—then an alchemy occurs whereby the historian, in a sense, becomes the history." Further on, Duncan writes, "Such a person never merely traces the outline of the past. Texts do not sit side by side on the shelf, but intermingle, entering into conflict and confluence with one another until the probable emerges from the impossible."[64] Janice attributes Duncan's theory to an idiosyncratic philosopher-historian and seems to see in it the musings of a man who has lost the capacity to separate what he does from what he writes about—someone who should be a reporter and chronicler of facts but who has inserted himself into the drama. Duncan, however, theorizes not so much heterodox disciplinary standards for the practice of history but rather concepts of history and historian impossible for such a discipline to even acknowledge, much less assimilate.

All of this comes to a head in *Finch*, where Duncan first appears as one of the dead bodies John Finch investigates at the start of the novel. As part of his investigation, Finch eats Duncan's memory bulb, a fruiting body produced from a corpse by a gray cap technique that allows its consumer to experience the past consciousness of the dead. Unlike previous memory bulbs, this one does not give Finch any access to a corpse's memory. Rather, it facilitates a conversation with Duncan inside his mind (although Finch is not yet aware of Duncan's identity). The memory bulb also allows Duncan to implant something of himself inside Finch as a means by which to emerge within the Ambergris of Finch's time from his travels throughout the larger text of which the city is made.

Just before and just after this emergence, Duncan has a further conversation with Finch in which he cryptically reveals who he is and explains much of what he has done and still plans to do. When Finch asks him what he will do next, Duncan replies, "I complete the mission. Time doesn't work the way we think it works. Not really. I'll go into the [Hoegbotton & Frankwrithe Zone] to pick up the trail. From there, I will journey years and worlds away and return. An army gathered with me.

I will be the beacon, the light, that guides them."[65] This army will consist of those who were lost in the Silence, some seven centuries before the events of *Finch*, and their descendants. Duncan further reveals that this attempt to defeat the gray caps is actually his second attempt. The first involved an attempt at changing the past as Samuel Tonsure. All of this intervention—involving a becoming-fungal that affords one the power to enter the text itself and move freely within it, and perhaps even write more of it—has been necessary, it seems, because conventional textuality, representation, and history are not up to the task: "The truth? None of my books ever changed anything. Nothing I did changed *anything*. I always tried, and I always failed."[66] Duncan had always tried to end the story, to complete it. However, he failed to recognize how the story—as a world, as that which means itself, as a material condition coextensive with textuality—is always already complete insofar as there are three Ambergris novels making up the sum total of Ambergris itself.

In his introduction to 2007's *Best American Fantasy, Volume 1*, VanderMeer notes, "There's no *real* end to narrative, just as there is no real end to the ways in which 'fantasy' elements can be put into the service of narrative."[67] Tolkien, along with so many of the fantasy writers who followed, understood all too well that, as Sam laments, the great stories never seem to end. There is always more to come, even if this "more" can never be narrated. However, Duncan Shriek reveals the incompleteness of narrative, rather than world, to be a function of the way humans retain a limited understanding of it—an understanding that insists that narrative reflect history as well as the material world to which it all too often binds itself in a logic of representation. This representation then devolves into textuality when humans discover how it always fails. Shriek elevates this failure, which seems inescapable, to being tantamount to escape itself—not because representation has finally achieved its goal of perfect mimesis but because books need not be bound to representation. They may embody their own materiality through their textuality. They may involve a fantastic materiality to the extent that textuality affords impossibility. Thus the fantasy elements VanderMeer deploys in Ambergris serve narrative less than a world building utterly colonized, funguslike, by textuality and the elements that constitute textuality. The Silence happens because characters can disappear in books without causes we understand to be possible. They return decades or centuries later from worlds unknown because time and space have no meaning in books. Duncan lives, or Duncan is reborn from a memory and the materiality described in and found in books, because that can happen in books. All of this impossibility, characteristic of secondary worlds in general, happens in books. This happening does not suggest the subcreation of a secondary world out there mirroring the primary world out there, but rather involves laws that contradict that world. This is the materialization of a textuality, a materiotextualization that is a worlding, an autoextension of the material and the textual with each other. Ambergris produces the impossible as a natural consequence of this worlding, the effect of a primal cause. The fear of falling into an endless criticality that denies the possibility of representation and the materiality of what might be represented depends on an assumption about the nothingness of textuality. This assumption tells us there is no way out—but in fact there may be a way.

4

THERE IS NOTHING BUT BORDER. THERE IS NO BORDER.

AREA X AND THE WEIRD PLANET

BORDERS AND BORDERING

The climactic moment in *Authority*, the second volume of the Southern Reach trilogy, comes as Control patrols the halls of the government agency he nominally directs.[1] Even as those who work there and report to him resist his authority in subtle and unsubtle ways, this space affords him a certainty, a comfort tantamount to complacency. No matter how many challenges and problems the Southern Reach facility presents to Control, it remains human. By way of the assumptions conditioning human knowledge, it remains distinct and distinguished from Area X, the agency's raison d'être. However, Area X, as a motivation for the Southern Reach, operates in a complex, often contradictory fashion: both as an object of inquiry and as a means of self-delusion. Publicly, the agency maintains a cover story for Area X about a "localized environmental catastrophe stemming from experimental military research."[2] Internally, the truth is both less complex and less explanatory: "About thirty-two years ago, along a remote southern stretch known by some as the 'forgotten coast,' an Event had occurred that began to transform the landscape and simultaneously caused an invisible border or wall to appear."[3] This passage may contain the sum total of what official human agencies have come to know about Area X before the beginning of the trilogy, and even later: something happened.

Moreover, it makes clear how the official cover story serves more than one purpose. In fact, it serves at least four convoluted purposes that fold over from outward-facing public relations to internal-facing mythopoesis. First, as implied, it excludes the public from the truth that there was an Event. It thereby creates an inside and an outside: a group who knows and can act, and a group who does not and cannot. Second, it conceals a deeper truth: even within the Southern Reach, no one understands the Event. This concealment reinforces the inside/outside binary but reframes the motivation for it in terms of a quest for further knowledge rather than in terms of a clear truth too dangerous to reveal, at least for the Southern Reach's purposes. Third, and following from this last point, the cover story allows the Southern Reach to mythologize its mission to and for itself. Even if no one yet understands Area X, the Southern Reach is determined to understand it, and by understanding it protect those who exist outside of the sphere of knowledge within which the Southern Reach positions itself. This third reason creates a cohesiveness to the inside (even if not everyone on the inside participates in this cohesion, as Control would be quick to note). Fourth, the cover story conceals something from the Southern Reach itself that many within the Southern Reach cannot fully face: there may be no progress to make with regard to understanding or explaining Area X, much less protecting the general public from it. The cover story, by virtue of being a story, conceals the utter absence of a meaningful story at all, and the impossibility of the Southern Reach moving from less knowledge to more knowledge, from here to there, from home to away and back again. If this cover story reveals anything, it declares, for the reader, the Southern Reach's irresistible, inescapable, and irreducible anthropocentrism, one indexing every event to human agency, force, and meaning. The cover story manifests and maintains the myth of ideal containment, of a border dividing the known from the unknown but knowable, the same from the different but potentially similar by virtue of an underlying sameness making comparison and progress possible.

Whether the outward-facing cover story works for the general public remains unclear; throughout the trilogy, the general public largely remains out of sight, an outside to the agency's inside. The director of the Southern Reach before Control, and the psychologist for and leader of the final expedition into Area X, thinks of the public as "people who were never allowed to see behind the curtain."[4] When the public does appear, exemplified by various locals from the towns near Area X, it manifests, in the gaze of the paranoid eyes of government agents who know too much and yet understand so little, as those who are not part of the story (as in the psychologist's statement) or those who must be incorporated into it. Drunks at bars and kids on the street become, in these eyes, willing and unwilling components of vast conspiracies, agents of surveillance and subjects of manipulation by those at the highest levels of power and by the material world in which they act.

The members of the general public thus become meaningful within the Southern Reach's mythopoesis, the story it tells about itself and about the materiality it investigates: a totalizing story that draws everything into itself under the assumption that everything can be made to fit within this inside. The public's understanding of Area X, and its credulity with regard to the lies surrounding Area X—the stories it might tell about itself and the materiality it interacts with, about its knowing and being in its own terms—remains entirely inconsequential to Control and those who work above and below him. The public's knowledge and desires have little purchase on the deeper mystery the Southern Reach penetrates every day, even if, at some point in the future, the truths behind this mystery might be revealed to the public so this public might be formally included on the inside of this mystery. For now, the pubic remains unknowingly related to this mystery as a potential inclusion. This potential to cross an abstract border, one that operates to separate the different from the same under the condition that everything different is potentially the same, demonstrates the degree to which the Southern Reach is beholden to a certain type of liberalism, one extending its own manner of knowing and being so everything and everyone can be afforded the "right" to be counted within it.

I turn below, where I demonstrate the dangers of the Southern Reach's liberalist/illiberalist binary under the threat of Area X, to the question of the general public, of those who experience effects without ever being a cause, who are subject to a condition unable to register their presence, who are on the ignorant outside vis-à-vis a knowledgeable inside. For now we must return to Control in the hallways of the Southern Reach, where he is about to confront the limitations inherent to the sort of borders humans rely on to create difference and invite sameness.

Control is preoccupied with two things. First, he believes that his assistant director may be undermining his authority in her loyalty to the previous director and the ideas about Area X the previous director lived by. Second, he has noticed the absence of the rotting honey smell that has plagued him during his tenure at the Southern Reach. The former preoccupation highlights the rampant anthropocentrism guiding this agency and, by extension, national security apparatuses and other human institutions generally. Even in the event of an Event, even within miles of a seemingly hostile force no one has been able to understand for more than three decades, personal loyalty and office politics dominate the thoughts of those in power. The latter preoccupation has little significance to Control, who assumes that the now-absent smell had something to do with a cleaning product used by the invisible janitorial staff. Control wanders through an office building dedicated to understanding something resistant to all attempts to understand it while thinking about human drama and a minor nuisance. Then this happens:

> He turned the corner into the corridor leading to the science
> division, kept walking under the florescent lights in a rehearsal
> of what he would say to Whitby, anticipating what Whitby
> might say back, or not say, feeling the weight of the man's
> insane manuscript.

> Control reached out for the large double doors. Reached
> for the handle, missed it, tried again.
> But there were no doors where there had always been
> doors before. Only wall.
> And the wall was soft and breathing under the touch of
> his hand.
> He was screaming, he thought, but from somewhere
> beneath the sea.[5]

It's difficult to do justice to this moment, stripped as it is of context, a moment that mirrors the aforementioned Event not only because it represents Area X establishing itself here and now, but more importantly because this establishment so easily defies the various techniques that have, to human observers such as Control and the reader, contained Area X to this point in the trilogy. In the first volume, *Annihilation*, characters and readers encountered Area X's weirdness on nearly every page. For characters and readers in that context, Area X may be difficult or impossible to understand, but it remains ideally and potentially accessible to human understanding insofar as its borders, both the geographical border described in the novel and the covers of the novel itself, contain it. By contrast, the human drama and human spaces Control inhabits in a separate novel called *Authority*, in all of their soporific mundanity, seem safe from such weirdness. Control is therefore unprepared for the manifestation of Area X within this banal, all too human world, within a novel of comparatively petty human conflicts. Readers are likewise unprepared, if to a lesser extent; they will have encountered the rotting honey smell in *Annihilation*, where the biologist "experience[s] a pinprick of escalation in the smell of rotting honey" just as she inhales the spores that initiate her monstrous transformation.[6]

This lack of preparedness involves a fundamental misunderstanding of Area X's border: a belief it exists along a line dividing one space or type of space from another in a larger homogeneous context affording progress and comparison. (Context is an explicit concern for the Southern Reach, which instructs members of the final expedition into Area X to "provide maximum context, so that anyone ignorant of Area X could understand our accounts."[7]). The border is naturally "invisible to the naked eye,"[8] but human architecture constructed along a line standing in for this border reinforces the idea of the border being here. Likewise, this architecture and the abstract line it realizes distinguishes this here from a there on the other side. As Control walks the corridors of the Southern Reach, the techniques and assumptions this architecture involves fail—not because the borders built according to their logics were overwhelmed by a siege perpetrated by a force lying beyond them but because their abstract lines have no purchase on and do not register with a space that is nothing but border.

As the former director dies within Area X, she recognizes the assumption of a border conforming to human expectations about borders as "a child's question. A question whose answer means nothing. There is nothing but border. There is no border."[9] In a theory-fiction engaging with the work of China Miéville, Roger Luckhurst offers seven weird theses, the sixth of which states, "The weird builds worlds precisely to breach them. It is (in) Breach."[10] Luckhurst's second sentence reveals the inadequacy of his first. This first sentence suggests the weird presents a comprehensible, complete, consistent, coherent world it then violates in some fashion. To the human character who lives in such a world, or to the human reader engaging with it, such might appear to be the case. However, the second sentence—which alludes to the mysterious agency in Miéville's *The City and the City* (2009) responsible for maintaining difference and punishing those who violate its mandate—suggests the weird is in violation of something, as would be the case when an individual transgresses a legal or social norm, but also is this violation—violation all the way down in the contextual absence of any norm actually being violated. Area X appears to violate its established border by way of irruption, but anyone who understands it to be doing so has been limited by assumptions about the nature of this border. Everyone, even Control, is aware of the dangers of such assumptions. When one member of his team says "something during their meeting about making assumptions about terminology," Control replies, "You mean like calling something a 'border'?"[11] Nonetheless, he fails to anticipate Area X's incursion into the Southern Reach building and the larger world outside of the border it had established for itself according to its own logics. Area X does not presuppose a complete world before violation because Area X is not an invasive force from a spatial outside or a temporal afterward. It is what already exists here around us, affecting us while remaining imperceptible to and unaffected by us. (The biologist fears how, in Area X, "the natural world around me had become a kind of camouflage." When Control is confronted with idea, he revealingly asks, "All of this is a disguise?"[12]) Area X does not wait out there for humanity to discover, contain, and affect it. It is already with us but unaffected by us because we constitutively cannot perceive or understand the manner in which it registers what we do. Neither human techniques, from architecture to critical thought, nor the invisible lines these techniques render visible have anything to do with Area X, which remains immune to logics that identify the known and the unknown so the latter may be contained by the former.

As he confronts the degree to which his assumptions have failed him, Control imagines he might wake up from the present horror, from what his senses tell him is happening and from what his mind tells him cannot be happening. He confuses this moment with another moment of crisis and hopes all of it will "dissolve into nothing and the walls of his cell would fall away and he would walk out into a world that was real. . . . Even though the texture of the wall felt like a manta ray from the aquarium: firm and smooth, with a serrated roughness but with more give, and behind it the sense of something vast, breathing in and out. A rupture into the world of the rotted honey smell, fading fast but hard to forget."[13] His mistake, and the reader's, has been his assumption that this border operates like those abstract Westphalian ones to which nations and individuals still cling. Such borders are drawn on a materiality that at best tolerates them as it plays a long game in which humanity's part, like the general public the Southern Reach patronizingly believes it protects, matters little.

Control's confrontation with Area X stands at the heart of VanderMeer's accomplishment in the Southern Reach trilogy, one that outstrips all of his fiction's previous accomplishments. Veniss, especially in "The City," presents a milieu lacking both borders and centering points, but it achieves its effects as much by way of vagueness and brevity as by positive description. Ambergris, especially in *Shriek: An Afterword*, presents space as always already inhabited by something the human can only perceive through monstrous transformation, but such transformation seems to be a two-way street. What Duncan Shriek discovers within the materialized textuality of the Ambergris novels he can bring back and share. Similar to Veniss and Ambergris, Area X fantasizes a world in which humanity must negotiate and establish its position and meaning according to logics at odds with inherited knowledge practices and the modes of being they afford, and at odds with its preestablished understandings of materiality and the truths it conditions. Area X thus offers another formulation of fantastic materiality in which critique and historicism, and all of the modern baggage they come with, fail.

With Area X, however, VanderMeer does away with even the residual humanism of his previous fiction. Area X is not a meerkat, a flesh dog, or a milieu made possible by the unintended consequences of science or capitalism. It will not be pacified or forestalled by deceleration, reversal, or even extinction. Area X is not a text, nor is it amenable to editing or even reading by a human who has understood the nature of his textual condition. It will not be understood or interpreted, reduced to something digestible by human intellect. Area X is something else, what has always already disrupted the processes by which borders are established between that and this, between one space or time and another space or time, between the human and whatever its other happens to be. Although Control's confrontation with Area X appears to describe the invasion of one space (the mundane office building, late capitalism, the security state) by another (Area X, the environment, geologic or cosmological timescales and spatiality), in fact it does something far stranger and more profound. It describes the becoming apparent of the a priori unacknowledged and unknowledgeable presence of what I term the weird planet. Whereas Veniss and Ambergris describe and push against and through the borders of human thought, where the same meets the different, Area X manifests a radical difference, an adifference or abdifference. This radical difference does not afford a collapse in which terms previously distinguished by abstract borders find one another and merge. It involves an uncontainable space that is nothing but a bordering without border, a limiting that cannot be limited.

The confrontation with the weird planet, which cannot be reciprocal according to any human technique, enjoins a rethinking of politics that does away with the uncanny, a politics of the *geos* as planet rather than on *geos* as earth. The geopolitics that comes of this rethinking operates within a border where difference is never conditioned by an underlying sameness. This border space makes impossible the distinction of one abstraction from another, a distinction requiring the assumption of a deeper condition of sameness making reciprocity possible. To this end, I turn next to a discussion of what the weird planet is and how it defies the logic of liberalism. Here Elizabeth A. Povinelli's understanding of liberalism in the context of what she calls geontopower[14] demonstrates the incommensurability of politics, in the conventional sense of the term, with the nonliving earth. From this discussion, I turn to a consideration of gothic and weird monsters, with Area X offering an example of the latter that overcomes certain shortcomings of other weird monsters still burdened by gothic assumptions. As much as it has come to be celebrated in recent years by critics such as Graham Harman and Mark McGurl, even in the old, haute weird we can find a residual anthropocentricism denying the strangeness Area X conveys. This anthropocentrism operates by way of an illiberalism opposed to liberalism, but one that still maintains the potential for the assimilation of difference in the context of underlying sameness. In contrast to the so-called cosmic indifference demonstrated by Lovecraft's various weird monsters, I argue Area X exhibits abdifference, a nonattitude involving a flight from abstract borders and the distinctions they afford. Finally, this discussion allows me to suggest a reading practice apposite fantastic materiality, which allows Area X and the otherworlds of the new weird to be themselves without reducing them to the norms established by our own physics. This reading practice is reflected in the experience of those who are most affected by Area X, the general public and its clearest exemplar, the lighthouse keeper, Saul Evans. Saul's transformation marks an important moment in the establishment of Area X, but it also makes clear how the weird planet has always already existed, and the human desire to mark the surface of the earth with abstract borders and measurements has always already failed.

THE WEIRD PLANET

Area X solicits innumerable responses from those who encounter it. Broadly speaking, these responses comprise on the one hand attempts to grasp Area X in its own terms, by way of clumsy language ill-equipped for such endeavors, and on the other hand explicit or implicit claims and conjectures about Area X that demonstrate a complete inability to think outside of inherited logics. Ghost Bird, the imperfect double of *Annihilation*'s biologist, who manifests outside of Area X before the start of *Authority* and returns to Area X with Control at the beginning of *Acceptance*, exhibits the former response. When she finally stands in the tower, she understands how

> Area X was only concentrated here, in this cramped space,
> on these stairs, in the phosphorescent words with which
> she had become so familiar. Area X was all around them;
> Area X was contained in no one place or figure. It was the
> dysfunction in the sky, it was the plant Control had spoken
> of. It was the heavens and the Earth. It could interrogate you
> from any position or no position at all, and you might not even
> recognize its actions as a form of questioning.[15]

As well as any passage in the trilogy, Ghost Bird's reverie conveys both Area X's ubiquity and pervasiveness as well as its capacity to inhumanly interact with the human. Ghost Bird, whose being in part derives from Area X's capacity to be everywhere at once and from its inhuman stance vis-à-vis the human, sharply contrasts with Control's mother, Jackie Severance, who exhibits the other type of response to Area X, one characteristic of the Southern Reach and its anthropocentrism. She describes to her son, born John Rodriguez and now known as Control, the manner in which the government has tried to deal with Area X:

Imagine a situation, John, in which you are trying to contain something dangerous. But you suspect that containment is a losing game. That what you want to contain is escaping slowly, inexorably. That what seems impermeable is, in fact, over time becoming very permeable. That the divide is more perforated than unperforated. And that whatever this thing is seems to want to destroy you but has no leader to negotiate with, no stated goals of any kind.[16]

Severance hints at the weird even as she exemplifies an inability to think without inherited, conventional terms and conditions. The lifelong spy and administrator cannot imagine Area X outside of a certain context or politics, one in which "containment" merely opposes something like uncontainment or noncontainment, and one where uncontainment or noncontainment serves as a starting point for containment. She recognizes and valorizes abstract borders, which render both the contained and the as-yet uncontained visible and intelligible for humans. To her these borders have real consequences, regardless of whether they have any material force, regardless of whether those on the other "side" of the "negotiation" respect them, understand their meaning for the human, or even recognize their existence.[17] She cannot imagine that such abstractions have no utility whatsoever except to those who think like her, just as she cannot imagine Area X has no goals or values. She seems on the verge of an epiphany, a leap into the weird. However, she cannot move beyond the border informed by her own mind and the inherited logics containing it.

Eugene Thacker theorizes the impasse at which Jackie Severance finds herself when he wonders whether we can think about the supernatural as neither an exception to a hard-and-fast physics nor as what simply coexists with and alongside physics: "The question I'd like to pose is whether there is a third level, in which the supernatural actually bears little or no relation to the natural, in which what is experienced by a human subject has no correlate in the world or in thought. . . . Here the supernatural has no positive content; it neither stands in relation to the natural, nor is it an autonomous entity in itself." In this form, "the supernatural is less about any relation to the natural, normative world, and more about the impossibility of this relation, or indeed, any relation at all."[18] Area X is this sort of supernature, one lacking positive content, one that cannot be thought by human logic. This is not to say, however, that it lacks force. Humans may experience Area X and even recognize that they are experiencing it, but they cannot affect it in return because the manner in which it registers such effects cannot be perceived or understood by human techniques. Although Steven Shaviro would remind us such experience may very well not be available to cognition even if it provides a condition for cognition,[19] the issue here, insofar as it is political, has to do with knowledge and containment of Area X rather than experience per se. It seems no amount of experience with or of Area X leads to any actual knowledge or containment. That is, Area X may "experience" the human. However, the human cannot register "Area X experiencing the human" in its thought. Therefore, the human cannot understand itself to have affected Area X. "Experience," "register," "understand," and "affect" are all human terms. Whatever processing of the human that Area X accomplishes, it takes place at scales the human cannot perceive or within folds the human cannot traverse—hence the human awareness of Area X when it materializes before an individual or group and the lack of awareness when it does not. It is always there nonetheless, but beyond the human sensorium, coextensive with a bordering against which human thought exerts no pressure and from which it therefore receives no feedback.

This nonfeedback—Area X's weirdness, a function of its abdifference—becomes a challenge to humanity's conception of itself and drives the Southern Reach's expeditions into Area X. The biologist summarizes the official version of this drive: *"Feed Area X but do not antagonize it, and perhaps someone will, through luck or mere repetition, hit upon some explanation, some solution, before the world* becomes *Area X."*[20] Grace describes the heterodox version of this drive adopted by the former Southern Reach director to whom she remains loyal: "She became obsessed with making it react.... She believed that nothing we had done had *pushed* whatever it is behind Area X. That it handled everything we did too easily. Almost without thought. If thought could be said to be involved."[21] Whatever its implementation, this desire for reaction, for evidence of something on the other side that not only registers human provocation but also registers this provocation in a manner the provocateur can register in return, fails. Moreover, it reveals what people such as the former director have in common with those they claim to despise, those they see as antithetical to their actual mission. (Of course such antithesis itself implies a boundary impossible to cross. Lack of common cause can be ameliorated by compromise or submission under the unspoken assumption that "cause" in general conditions disagreement.)

Lowry, a survivor of the first expedition into Area X, someone who has risen through the ranks of the Southern Reach and beyond, fears the boredom of a world in which "they win," where "they" seems to designate Area X's agency and subjectivity.[22] The former director scoffs at this logic:

> As if people would be living in "that world" at all, which was
> what any of the evidence foretold, or kept foretelling, as if there
> were nothing worse than being bored and the only point of
> the world people already lived in was to find ways to combat
> boredom, to make sure "all the moments," as Whitby put it
> when he went on about parallel universes, might be accounted
> for in some way, so minds wouldn't fill up with emptiness that
> they bifurcated to have more capacity to be bored.[23]

Boredom involves a drive to other, a drive to produce or recognize a difference against which the self can be defined. It asserts itself in a space of nondifference or indifference amenable to potential differentiation. Area X's weirdness effaces self by way of the indistinct and indistinguishing border it involves, a border entirely congruent with it and therefore with everything else. This liquidation of antagonism bespeaks a weird politics outside of the Western anthropocentric politics based on the distinction between such differences as friend and enemy.[24] Likewise, Area X suggests a form of border that is material and yet intangible, and intangible without being abstract.

Horror in its various forms has long sought to describe what remains fundamentally beyond the human, and in the last decade critics and theorists of horror have increasingly sought a vocabulary to discuss this beyond. Thacker refers to the planet, which lies beyond humanly inhabitable worlds and the scientifically measurable earth, to designate the characteristics of where we live "that are not accounted for, not measured, and that remain hidden and occulted." He continues, "Anything that reveals itself does not reveal itself in total. This remainder, perhaps, is the 'Planet.'"[25] Luckhurst argues that as a concept, the uncanny's Freudian and therefore anthropocentric roots compromise its utility with regard to the contemporary world. In contrast to the "unhomeliness" of gothic horror, "*the weird has no home to start with. No oikos, no pure originary state. Only non-Euclidean folds and refolds.*"[26] The uncanny moves back and forth between home and away, between spaces contained within abstractly established borders; the weird effaces such categorization altogether. The weird may move, but it never departs from one place or arrives at another because it defies the very concept of place as a delimitation of materiality.

Adapting Thacker's planet to Luckhurst's weird, we might say Area X's refusal to reveal itself fully to the human does not indicate there is more to it, a complete or coherent totality that might be but is not (yet) being revealed. Area X does not shift between presence and absence, or even partial presence and partial absence. It knows nothing of partialness or wholeness because it can be neither analyzed nor contained. It is there all along, too big and too close to see. As the biologist puts it, "When you are too close to the center of a mystery there is no way to pull back and see the shape of it entire."[27] Area X involves a distortion of scale by which the human stands both atop and within Area X even as it traverses and swallows the human whole. It is what remains when the human finds itself in a place that is not and never was its home. In *Acceptance*, this distortion, this anti-*oikos*, reveals itself to the last survivors within Area X: "'We're not on Earth,' Ghost Bird said. We cannot be on Earth. 'Not with that much distortion of time. Not with the things the biologist saw.' Not if they wanted to pretend that there were rules in place, even if the rules had been obscured, made unclear, withheld."[28] Area X is not on earth because no border on a surface can contain it. Area X does not distort a given reality but rather is distortion generally, a materiality defined by distortion. Area X is already this, already here, and already now. Everything and everywhere and every-when—in short, Area X—cannot be home because it lacks the totality that abstract borders provide.

Thus, in contrast to the uncanny *oikos*, Area X offers a weird *geos* traversing, suffusing, and finally manifesting within what has been assumed as home.[29] This *geos* is a condition for absolute difference, a space within which nonrelation and abdifference obtain because it does not assume the sameness on which abstract borders, such as those of the Westphalian variety, are drawn. Povinelli's understanding of geontopower suggests how human borders, such as those between this form of life and that form of life, or between this side and that side, assume this sameness within which difference can be defined. Povinelli takes issue with biopower, a concept naming the processes by which life itself has come to be the focus of political governance, especially insofar as various forms of life are determined to be worth living and saving or not worth living or saving, which is to say how distinctions are made among those who are understood to be alive with regard to the value of their lives.[30]

Of late this concept, and the related concept of the biopolitical, has come under fire for any number of provincialisms. Jeffrey Nealon reveals how it limits considerations of life to animal life, to the exclusion of plants and other forms further from the human.[31] Alexander Weheliye demonstrates the limitations of Foucault's and Agamben's understanding of biopolitics with regard to race.[32] Thacker, while not focused specifically on the biopolitical or biopower, makes clear how perhaps the longest standing and most constitutive problem for philosophy is the question of what life is.[33] All of these discussions—of the necessity of thinking about life in all of its manifestations, of the necessity of thinking about racial difference and how racial others are included or excluded within the political, of how to understand life as both a characteristic of individual beings as well as a general principle manifesting in diverse forms of being—remain relevant and crucial to the present argument. However, Povinelli's geontopower bears directly on the question of the weird planet and its abdifference I am raising here, especially as it defies the liberal tendency to see every difference as a potential sameness. She writes, "The simplest way of sketching the difference between geontopower and biopower is that the former does not operate through the governance of life and the tactics of death but is rather a set of discourses, affects, and tactics used in late liberalism to maintain or shape the coming relationship of the distinction between Life and Nonlife."[34] With geontopower, Povinelli demonstrates how attempts to save the earth, whether explicitly for the humans who live there or for the earth itself, fall victim to a flawed inclusionary politics which insists everyone and everything be drawn inside, into the same political sphere and accorded the same set of political rights, each determined by a Western metaphysics that "measure[s] all forms of existence by the qualities of one form of existence (*bios, zoe*)." This liberalism, predicated by an implicit claim about "life (as understood by Western modes of thought) as the measure of all things," produces absurdities, such as questions of whether the land can vote on how it is used, not used, improved, or destroyed.[35]

Claims that Area X might have values—that it might be negotiated with, that it might participate in some form of conversation, that it might be understood—exemplify such absurdity. As a manifestation of the weird planet, Area X is an area, but not in the conventional senses of either what is set aside for a particular use (as in politics) or of a surface measured by regular units (as in science). Rather, it cannot be set aside because there is no aside; it cannot be for a particular use because it is immanent to every use by way of its constant unaffected and unaffectable presence.[36] It is what cannot be made regular. Even its encroachment on the rest of the world operates outside of regularity. The previous director of the Southern Reach tells the biologist in *Annihilation*, "The border is advancing. For now, slowly, a little bit more every year. In ways you wouldn't expect. But maybe soon it'll eat a mile or two at a time."[37] However, the biologist, who has been infected by Area X and grows more attuned to it every day, finds "this statement too limiting, too ignorant. . . . We had come to think of the border as this monolithic wall, but if members of the eleventh expedition had been able to return without our noticing, couldn't other things have already gotten through?"[38] Thus its encroachment must be a manifestation, even if this manifestation is of what is already there.

This manifestation takes place within a geopolitics that understands the earth as a neutral surface on which abstract lines might be drawn to divide one national group from another or erased to reconnect such groups, and within a science that believes it can measure things and make them available to human thought. Area X is a space both of and not of this world, something both containing and contained by the earth, a space obviating the problem of where one stands when one contemplates the object for the fact that such contemplation can have no purchase on the weird planet. One can already be in Area X before one even enters it, as when the biologist states at the top of the topographical anomaly known as the tower, "I think we all realized that only now had we truly entered Area X."[39] Likewise, the director of the Southern Reach before Control recognizes how even getting to the tower requires moving across internal, unmarked borders: "There are other borders within Area X, other gauntlets, and you have passed through one to get to the topographical anomaly."[40]

Area X reveals a certain limitation to the way we have thought of the Anthropocene: as another human construction and as another way to assert our agency in the face of scales defying even the logic of scale. In the short term, humans may affect the weird planet, but the weird planet does not notice or react in terms the human can comprehend. The weird planet is not even indifferent. To be indifferent, it would have to be different than us, positioned to be impartial with respect to an other. To be indifferent, to state that "it's all the same to me," requires an initial difference to be overcome. To be indifferent, even in the cosmic sense that weird fiction has taken as its hallmark since Lovecraft, involves the uncanny: the return to or arrival at sameness after a departure based in otherness.[41] The weird planet is adifferent, abdifferent—outside of or fleeing from notions of difference.[42] This is precisely its terror: it is there already without being detectable, it affects us because it is us, and it cannot be affected by us because we are already it.

When we think as humans, when we draw borders as humans, we assume we know what lies on this side of the border. We also assume that what lies on the other side may be eventually contained by becoming what is on this side—or at least kept at bay as itself on the other.

When we think as humans, we fail to acknowledge the problem of the border generally, how a border might function less as a line drawn on a flat surface than as a sphere in which we already move, or as a radical flatness already containing us.[43] Area X, whose border is nowhere and everywhere, which is entirely made up of border, makes no such assumption. As Povinelli writes with regard to what she calls Nonlife, Area X is "affect without intention and is affected without the intentional agency to affect." When we interact with it, it does not register this interaction and returns to us no comprehensible or usable information about the interaction or the fallout from it. As such, Area X is "inert, no matter the force with which it hurtles itself through space or down a hill."[44] The weird planet will destroy us eventually, but not for revenge, and certainly not because it desires destruction. The weird planet, Area X, will destroy us because it desires nothing; it is materiality, and materiality is inexorable.

MONSTROSITY: DIFFERENT, INDIFFERENT, ABDIFFERENT

Area X may well destroy humanity, but this outcome does not call for pessimism. Likewise, it does not enjoin a nonpolitical stance ignoring humanity and humaneness in the name of survival. Rather, it requires a rethinking of politics that recognizes and accepts the weird and does away with the uncanny, a politics of the planet rather than on the earth, that is the border rather than what relies on a border: a politics of abdifference. In order to grasp what such a politics entails, we must first understand the limitations of what has been called the weird monster's indifference.

In a recent work of cultural history, Leo Braudy identifies four types of modern monsters, each of which appeared sometime after the mid-eighteenth century in reaction to the increased secularization of the world and as means by which the contradictions of capitalism and other modern institutions could be sublimated: "the monster from nature (like King Kong), the created monster (like Frankenstein), the monster from within (like Mr. Hyde), and the monster from the past (like Dracula)."[45]

In a manner similar to a few of the categories in Jorge Luis Borges's "certain Chinese encyclopedia,"[46] these seem, at least in one case, self-containing. Clearly they at least overlap. Hyde (and his relative, the werewolf) emerges from within the human as an avatar of a nature repressed by modern social norms and scientific advancement. More importantly, however, we should understand that all of these monsters are created; Frankenstein's monster and other automata (such as robots, golems, and artificial intelligences) are simply the most obvious examples of created monsters insofar as material human labor produces them. Monsters that come from nature, monsters that come from the past, and monsters that come from within are nonetheless created, namely by way of modernity and history, by way of a mind-set that states, "We are no longer *primitive*. We are *modern*. History has happened." In short, they are created by an abstract difference taking various forms: now versus then, here versus there, this versus that, home versus away.

However, because they are created, these monsters and the borders that define them endlessly shift. What is home can become an away or an unhome through a monstrous invasion. Thus "home" will always have a double meaning: on the one hand it is the place from which the modern human commences and to which it hopes to return, the space it has defined for itself that is opposed to the rest of the world. On the other hand it is the primal home, the nature humanity has already left behind by way of prior commencement and previous border production. Thus these monsters always both turn toward the home, the space the modern has produced for itself, and disrupt it, while at the same time returning the modern to its home in the premodern world it had hoped to permanently leave behind. (In fact, the former disruption is precisely the latter enforced return.) Despite how far-reaching their destruction seems, however, these monsters wreak an irreducibly local havoc. They can only ever affect part of a whole because what they affect has nothing to do with space, simply understood. They may maraud in spaces as small as haunted houses and as large as London (as with Dracula and Hyde), New York City (as with King Kong), or even the Northern Hemisphere (as with Frankenstein's monster), but their true victims are only ever those bound to historicist, critical, scientific, and rational thought. Beyond these modern humans are those whose subjectivities are cast—nearly always in racist and/or misogynistic terms—as irrational, premodern, or primitive, and therefore outside the inside, other to the self, premodern to the modern. These groups, such as the indigenous islanders in *King Kong* or the Transylvanians in *Dracula*, remain in the thrall of older epistemologies. They may fear monsters, but these monsters do not produce in them the sort of crisis experienced by the modern hero, often a white, upper-class, Protestant man. To this modern hero, the return of the repressed, the threat to his home, and the threat to "home" him, constitute an attack not so much on his progress but on the notion of progress generally. Thus, no matter how large gothic monsters' theaters of operations, their most profound effects remain local, limited to the epistemological space inhabited by those who call themselves modern. These monsters may represent a physical or spiritual threat to those who provide Euro-Americans with their cultural, racial, and historical others, but they can never challenge what these others are and must always be.

The weird monster in its most extreme form does not function within a logic that makes political, cultural, racial, or other abstract distinctions through border production. For this reason, Braudy's exclusion of this form of monster is frustrating but unsurprising—frustrating because of the opportunities he misses to theorize our contemporary situation, unsurprising because it reveals the extent to which our thought remains bound to certain conventions even when it seeks to theorize things outside of them. There is at least one extraordinary virtue to Braudy's exclusion of the weird, however. His infrequent references to H. P. Lovecraft, which draw Lovecraft's monsters into the gothic and the uncanny, demonstrate how even the haute weird, valorized again and again for its cosmic indifference by contemporary speculative philosophies and McGurls's cultural geology, sometimes relies on the remnants of modernity's enthusiasm for producing borders. In one of only three references to Lovecraft, Braudy connects him to the gothic tradition. In a passage about how film and other visual media transform the nature of the monster in the twentieth century, Braudy writes, "The gothic emphasis on the inability to describe the truly horrific—the awesome ineffability of the demonic—a tradition still honored in the twentieth century by writers like M. R. James and H. P. Lovecraft—was augmented by another of the new technologies, radio, which invited the reader into an otherwise invisible world filled by one's own imaginings." In a later passage, Braudy notes how Lovecraft's monsters tend to be related to "alien groups he feared personally: women, Jews, immigrants, foreigners of all sorts, the list is long."[47] These references to Lovecraft tell us little about him or his fiction, and in the context of Braudy's overall argument, they matter far less than his claims about, for example, horror in visual media more generally.

However, despite their brevity and relative unimportance in the context of Braudy's history, these two passages force us to recognize the difficulty even weird writers have had in divesting themselves of human abstraction. In Lovecraft's case, this difficulty derives from a conscious racism rather than only from unconscious assumptions imbricated in anthropocentric thought.[48] This case provides an opportunity to better understand the limits of liberalism by way of liberalism's opposite. Whereas liberalism seeks to include everyone, or even everything, within its narratives and thereby grant everyone and everything equal rights, illiberalism draws a border across which stand various others who and what will not be granted those rights. Nonetheless, the abstract nature of this border produces its own transgressions. Whether liberalism finally wins in specific cases or in general is beside the point; every other is potentially the same, every difference is potentially assimilated. A further examination of the weirdness of Lovecraft's monsters and how his racism undermines this weirdness will help to demonstrate the stakes for my discussion of Area X and what I am calling the weird planet and the geopolitics thereof.

The weirdness of Lovecraft's monsters involves, in general, a disavowal of inherited notions of monstrosity. In Miéville's argument,[49] the weird monster offers an entirely new teratology, one that rejects stately ghosts, aristocratic undead, anthropomorphic animals, and irreligious demons. The weird monster, which Lovecraft dates to the "lean, dwarfish, and hairy" ghosts of M. R. James,[50] eschews reference to the history of monsters as inherited from the legends or mythologies of Europe and the United States. Along with this refusal of extant forms, Lovecraft suggests that extant terminology fails in the face of these monsters, even if this terminology is bent toward such description in the end. Lovecraft's narrators are well known for avowing that Cthulhu and shoggoths, and even the spaces in which these entities can be found, cannot be described. At the same time, as Graham Harman exhaustively demonstrates, Lovecraft nonetheless consistently offers precise, if impossible, descriptions of these monsters.[51] Consider the famous description of the Cthulhu statue in "The Call of Cthulhu" (1928):

> If I say that my somewhat extravagant imagination yielded
> simultaneous pictures of an octopus, a dragon, and a human
> caricature, I shall not be unfaithful to the spirit of the thing.
> A pulpy, tentacled head surmounted a grotesque and scaly
> body with rudimentary wings; but it was the general outline
> of the whole which made it most shockingly frightful. Behind
> the figure was a vague suggestion of a Cyclopean architectural
> background.[52]

Also consider the description of the shoggoths in *At the Mountains of Madness*, as depicted by the murals of the Old Ones:

> Formless protoplasm able to mock and reflect all forms and
> organs and processes—viscous agglutinations of bubbling
> cells—rubbery fifteen-foot spheroids infinitely plastic and
> ductile—slaves of suggestion, builders of cities—more and
> more sullen, more and more intelligent, more and more
> amphibious, more and more imitative—Great God! What
> madness made even those blasphemous Old Ones willing to
> use and to carve such things?[53]

Again, Lovecraft's narrators often insist on the impossibility of rendering these monsters in human language, but they nonetheless proceed with an attempt to do so.[54] As such, Lovecraft seems far less interested in what Braudy calls "the awesome ineffability of the demonic" than he is with the limitations of human knowledge and the techniques that are part and parcel of this knowledge. More precisely, he is interested in

monsters who do not so much challenge this or that idea, this or that category, but in monsters who challenge the very notion of "category" and
the thought that produces it generally—monsters that both come from
some outside and remain there, inaccessible to a humanity that nonetheless experiences their effects.

However, the difficulty of presenting the weird in language—in
describing what remains uncontainable by human thought and the borders defining it by way of one of those techniques most clearly productive
of those borders and the inside they contain—returns us to Thacker's
attempt to understand the supernatural as something other than an
exception to physics or a complement/supplement to physics. Benjamin
Noys articulates this problem in Lovecraft as follows: in the conflict
between, first, the fact of time and, second, extinction and a speculation
about a suspension of natural law, "we seem to be left with the paradox
of a horror based on science that threatens to proceed through an insipid
anti-scientific mysticism." Noys continues, "Lovecraft's actual solution,
at least in his great texts, was more inventive: the suspension of natural
laws would produce a new materialism which liberates us into the experience of the horror of time in its suspension from any law and any relation."[55] Noys rearticulates this point with reference to Lovecraft's "The
Shadow Out of Time" (1936), "Here it is a matter of what kind of object
constitutes the shadow that falls from the outside—not a mystical outside of completed alterity, the *tout Autre*, but a material 'outside' which
does not respond to the effect of law or to any correlation or relation to
humanity."[56] For Noys, Lovecraft does away with the supernatural altogether and formulates a material outside even as this material outside
remains beyond the reach of humanity, that which affects the human
without being affected by it. Indeed, one of the hallmarks of Lovecraft's
monsters is their cosmic indifference, their idiocy. They do not register
the presence of humanity, which remains so far beneath them as to be
imperceptible, or at least imperceptible in terms of humanity's awareness and understanding of it.

The problem is that it is not always precisely true that this impercep-
tibility indicates a lack of relation between these monsters and humanity, and Braudy's reminder about Lovecraft's racism demonstrates as

much. Lovecraft's outside may exist beyond the knowledge and practice of the scientists and other academics who encounter its effects, beyond the capacity of anyone on the inside of a certain abstract border to affect. However, it relates to the racial and ethnic others who populate, for example, "The Call of Cthulhu" and "The Dunwich Horror" (1929), not to mention lesser fictions, such as the execrable "The Horror at Red Hook" (1927).[57] Lovecraft's racism, misogyny, anti-Semitism, and xenophobia—rather than some fidelity to a gothic alacrity for the indescribable—render his monsters uncanny for the fact that these attitudes reveal an assumed relationship between monstrosity and localized groups (even if these groups do not appear in a single geographical place), groups whose locality stands opposed to the locality in which modernity and rationality obtain. The practitioners of the Cthulhu cult, the inhabitants of Innsmouth—such characters in Lovecraft's fiction identify with monsters and seek monstrosity as a means to power or self-preservation, in contrast to the rational white male scientists who understand the threat that these monsters embody to the modern world. In Lovecraft, these monsters do not threaten those who are already monstrous, those who are already outside of modernity, to the same extent or in the same manner as they threaten those who are inside modernity. Thus Lovecraft's monsters remain gothic to the extent they remain local, contained by a border separating the same from the different, one that may be crossed in order to transform one space into the other. Understanding this limitation of the weird, how it has been deployed in the service of an abstract border running within the human in order to claim victim status for the powerful and to justify the torture and oppression of the marginalized, has implications for our understanding of Area X as an example of fantastic materiality and as a counterweight to our understandings of the Anthropocene.

To a far greater extent than Lovecraft's monsters, Area X manifests the truly weird. As such, it can in no way be a representation of the Anthropocene if by Anthropocene we mean "a true material thing extant in the world and usable as a measure for the accuracy of this or that fiction." Area X produces and deploys an encroaching indistinction beyond even the Anthropocene's forceful production of a human totality experiencing it regardless of race, gender, nationality, sexuality, ability, or (to a lesser extent) economic class. As an exemplification of the weird planet and as the bearer of geopolitics, Area X flouts certain aspects of how the Anthropocene has been conceptualized. In chapter 1, I discussed the Anthropocene as an historical period not because it can be precisely dated or because it has any relationship to human meaning other than what human beings construct for it. Rather, the Anthropocene is an historical period (and the frame for, rather than a referent of, the Southern Reach trilogy) because it enjoins a response from cultural producers and critics outstripping all other objects of inquiry. We must respond to the Anthropocene, "feed it without antagonizing it, in the hopes that perhaps someone will, through luck or mere repetition, hit on some explanation, some solution, before the world becomes Anthropocene" (to repurpose the biologist's summary of the Southern Reach's mission).[58]

However, Area X defies every attempt to provoke it into providing feedback meaningful to human beings. Human beings die in, and because of, Area X. They are transformed into owls, dolphins, and monsters. In short, they are affected by Area X. However, they never understand what has been done to them, or even if their provocations are the cause of what has been done to them. They are affected by Area X without affecting it because whatever effect they have on it cannot be registered as such. Such registration would require containment, the imposition of an abstract border around an object or concept that affords the registration, comprehension, understanding of this object or concept for the human who produces those borders. Rather than being such an abstract border, which implies a home known on this side and an away unknown on the other, as well as the possibility of transforming each into its opposite, Area X's border is a bordering of the human such that the human is always contained and delimited without being able to produce a reciprocal containment or delimitation. Area X can only exist in fiction, and it can only be a fantastic materiality. Our attempts to understand it should not involve the containment that comes with understanding it in terms of representation. We should allow ourselves to be affected by it without needing to affect it. This is not a call for indifference with regard to a global catastrophe, but rather a call for abdifference with regard to a fiction irreducible to reality or the rules we understand to govern it.

PLANETARY BODIES

Scholars of the weird and new weird mainly agree that the latter takes a more explicitly political stance than the former.[59] In chapter 1, I discussed the problem of the weird's residual critical stance and claimed the new weird's politics are bound up with its monsters, a discussion I have expanded in this chapter. Following from this expansion, the problem of the former and the promise of the latter can be reframed in terms of the gap between indifference and abdifference. Indifference (and its augmented form, cosmic indifference) effectively describes an attitude held by the universe or the powers within it toward humanity and other similarly inferior forms of existence. Its shortcomings are both specific and general. Specifically, Lovecraft's racism demonstrates the inherent interest humanity takes in its world, its desire to make the world according to its own local understandings of reality or materiality. This interest and this desire operate on the level of politics conventionally understood, which is to say at a human scale. Cosmic indifference, as deployed in Lovecraft, similarly betrays the impossibility of disinterest even as it posits an uncaringness for a humanity understood as what has no essential meaning within an inconceivably vast expanse of time and space. At the very least, indifference suggests, with or without its modifier, a potential interest one might take but has not yet taken, if not an interested disinterestedness that has already been established. Just as boredom can be overcome by the introduction of difference, indifference might proceed to interest with the introduction of something new or alien—knowledge, for example, or a type of person one hates. The "ab-" in abdifference does not amplify or otherwise augment a concept of indifference. Rather, it designates a movement away, a constantly renewed flight from difference and from everything particular and toward nothing in particular, a movement without trajectory within a space without markers. It is a nonattitude, a nonrelation, a means of identifying the measureless gap between the human with its knowledge practices and the weird planet without a capacity to be known.

This gap appears not only in the Southern Reach trilogy, where it divides humans and their agencies from Area X, but also between the reader in this world and the otherworlds of new weird fiction. As my arguments throughout this book have made clear, no critical stance or historicism can overcome this gap. The gap is one between a given materiality whose norms become a measure for what fiction ought to do—what it ought to represent on the one hand, and a fantastic world whose materiality produces entirely other norms on the other. The new weird and the Southern Reach trilogy require abdifferent reading practices. Readers of such fiction must not be indifferent; they must not say, "It's all the same to me." Readers must not be uncaring, lacking concern and therefore willing to forgo attention. The Anthropocene demands attention, and even if Area X cannot be reduced to a representation of the Anthropocene, we will have learned nothing by way of fantastic materiality if we mistake abdifference for unconcern, lack of care, or inattention. Rather, an abdifferent reading practice requires a care or concern that allows fiction to be itself, to be fantastic and develop a nonexistent, impossible materiality: a care not to care, a concern not to concern ourselves as people who live here and are bound by the laws we assume to govern us. It must move away from the difference produced by and necessary for critique, which measures the success of a fiction by how well it reflects a given reality. However, as I suggest above, this flight does not imply despair; nor does it involve giving up. Rather, it involves imagining conditions that afford new ways of thinking and that do not assume a stable, grounding reality. To fantasize, or fictionalize, materiality does not mean to abandon oneself to fantasy but to abandon the fantasy that we always already are able to know and are able to question such knowing.

The characters of the Southern Reach trilogy model abdifference. Some of these characters seem to intuit their movement away from difference and abstract borders and into a bordering without measurement and beyond use. Even before the biologist enters Area X, she tells her husband how, during her late-night outings, she goes nowhere even as she thinks, "*Everywhere.*"[60] Sometime after Control's confrontation with

Area X in the hallways of the Southern Reach facility, he feels yearnings that "now went in all directions and no direction at all. It was an odd kind of affection that needed no subject, that emanated from him like invisible rays meant for everyone and everything."[61] In the trilogy's final lines, the dying former director of the Southern Reach realizes that Area X is done with her, that it will question her no longer (if questioning is the right term for what it does):

> You are still there for a moment, looking out over the sea
> toward the lighthouse and the beautiful awful brightness of
> the world.
>   Before you are nowhere.
>   Before you are everywhere.[62]

Other characters, and even the same characters at other moments, participate in abdifference without being aware of doing so. As I have spent considerable time focused on the latter, I here turn to the former, whose planetary bodies manifest a brightness that reveals the ecstatic nonrelation with the weird planet, the concern with Area X.

Because they do not know and are denied the opportunity to know, the public for whom the Southern Reach ostensibly maintains its cover story about Area X is the first population rendered vulnerable to Area X, something that the pre–Southern Reach intelligence community sees in the history of strange occurrences along what is known as the "forgotten coast" and that it encourages by way of a mysterious group known as the Séance & Science Brigade. The trilogy largely takes place along this forgotten coast, an area of what a representationalist understanding of the trilogy—in which Area X is the Anthropocene and the Southern Reach a branch of the CIA—would claim to be the United States, likely Florida.[63] (Whatever its relation to given reality, it is never identified by any other name; nor are the states in which it resides and the nation in which those states exist named. This lack of reference is already suggestive of a nonrepresentationalism and therefore a lack of traditional political aims.) When the Event produced Area X and the border "came down," as numerous officials put it, the inhabitants of the forgotten coast became locked behind it, their fate unknown. As the biologist thinks to herself, seemingly parroting the official story, "People had still lived there, on what amounted to wildlife refuge, but not many, and they tended to be the tight-lipped descendants of fisherfolk. Their disappearance might have seemed to some a simple intensifying of a process begun generations before."[64]

In some respects—for example, their lack of economic viability, their want for the sorts of institutions most Americans take for granted, their distance from cultural centers—the denizens of the forgotten coast might remind the reader of the sort of allegedly premodern people who populate gothic horror novels and warn modern protagonists of the dangers of vampires, witches, or werewolves. Indeed, the forgotten coast seems to be a focal point for superstition: "Strangeness was nothing new for Failure Island. If you listened to Old Jim, or some of the other locals, the myths of the forgotten coast had always included that island, even before the latest series of attempts at settlement had failed."[65] In the nearby town of Hedley, where Control lives in the trilogy's present, we find another staple of the gothic and the potential for a return of the repressed that might unhome the scientists and administrators of the Southern Reach: "Back in the day the liquor store had been a department store. Long before Hedley was built, there had been an indigenous settlement here, along the river—something his father had told him—and the remains of that, too, lay beneath the facade of the liquor store."[66] In an even more explicit reference to this sort of gothic mentality, Control thinks about the nature of the forgotten coast "before the border came down" in terms of the "kind of 'strange doings' alluded to by hard-working bearded fishermen in old horror movies as they stared through haunted eyes at the unforgiving sea."[67] The forgotten coast and the people who live there seem to provide the other to the Southern Reach's self, an outside to an inside, and an example of a liberal/illiberal binary according to which politics operates by creating differences via abstract borders.

It is possible, of course, to read this thread of the trilogy according to representationalist strategies and the politics such strategies articulate, as does Siobhan Carroll. Carroll writes, with regard to Control's

musings about the destruction of an indigenous settlement by capitalist progress, that "indigenous ways of ecological thought can no longer
be recovered by the characters inhabiting VanderMeer's late capitalist
world, nor do alternative forms of community exist to offer them potential escapes from the Capitalocene."[68] History, it seems, has gone too
far to allow for the return of this particular repressed. In contrast to this
reading, however, one premised on abdifference, on the acknowledgment that Area X is not the Anthropocene and that the trilogy does not
take place on earth at all, yields quite different results. What happened
on the forgotten coast involves an intensification of long-standing processes, as the biologist recognizes. However, the processes in question,
those causing the forgotten coast and its inhabitants to disappear behind
the border, are not historical; nor are they the machinations of capitalism, whatever Control's story about the layers of buying and selling built
over the bodies of indigenous people might suggest. The Southern Reach
trilogy instead describes the process by which Area X intensifies, by
which it completes a certain stage in its concentration along the forgotten coast and anticipates its future manifestation in the Southern Reach
(and everywhere else).

The lighthouse keeper, Saul Evans, whose encounter with a spiral of
light produces the first adumbration of Area X in the form of a brightness other characters would come to experience and fail to understand,
exemplifies this process. The reader first encounters him in a photograph
discovered and studied by the biologist in *Annihilation*, but his most powerful appearance in this text comes near its end, when the biologist finally
encounters the Crawler, a monster that ascends and descends the stairs of
the tower while writing words on the tower's wall comprising entire alien
ecologies. These words produce the spores that infect the biologist and
initiate her own transformation. In this encounter, the biologist, who can
read the words on the tower walls as words but not in terms of the weird
nonrepresentationalism in which they participate, is read by the Crawler:
"Apparently I was words it could understand," she thinks to herself. She
then looks at the Crawler and sees in it, "barely visible, the face of a man,
hooded in shadow and orbited by indescribable things [she] could think
of only as his jailers." She continues her observation:

The man's expression displayed such a complex and naked
extremity of emotion that it transfixed me. I saw on those
features the endurance of an unending pain and sorrow, yes, but
shining through as well a kind of grim satisfaction and *ecstasy.*
I had never seen such an expression before, but I recognized
that face. . . . The lighthouse keeper had not aged a day since that
photograph was taken more than thirty years ago. This man who
now existed in a place none of us could comprehend.[69]

Saul's movement to this place, which is not a movement because he is
already there, and which does not involve a place because this "there"
is an area without measure or use, begins in *Acceptance.* Saul, working
outside the lighthouse he keeps along the forgotten coast, notices "something glittering from the lawn." When he looks more closely, he sees
what seems to be "a tiny shifting spiral of light." As he reaches for it, he
becomes faint and tries to pull his hand away. "But it was too late. He felt
a sliver enter his thumb" that leaves no trace of entry.[70] When the reader
next encounters Saul, several chapters later, he is contemplating the
nature of bodies: "Bodies could be beacons, too, Saul knew. A lighthouse
was a fixed beacon for a fixed purpose, a person was a moving one. But
people still emanated light in their way, still shone across the miles as a
warning, an invitation, or even just a static signal. People opened up so
that they became a brightness, or they went dark."[71] The trilogy suggests
Area X may not (only) manifest here or there by way of some geologic
or cosmological process, but may use bodies as portals. Saul's body here
begins the process of becoming the first such portal.

Decades after Saul begins his transformation and calls Area X
forth, a scientist at the Southern Reach named Whitby may inaugu-
rate the process leading to Control's confrontation: Control "realized
then, or at some point later, that maybe Whitby wasn't just crazy. That
Whitby had become a breach, a leak, a door into Area X, expressed as
an elongated equation over time."[72] However, the process by which
bodies become beacons, by which they develop their brightness,
never represents an absolute origin for Area X or the penetration of a
border-delimiting world by something beyond that border. Rather, it

represents the intensification or concentration of something already present; it represents the rendering apparent of the measureless gap of abdifference against the background of a materiality that does not condition a potential for sameness.

Here we discover the profundity of fantastic materiality in the revelation that ubiquitous materiality does not warrant the claim that everything is material in the same way. Povinelli's severing of life from nonlife, from what was never alive and never can be, by way of her conception of geontopower is crucial here, not only for what it makes clear about how marginalized groups (especially indigenous groups) become marginalized but also because it demonstrates the limits of liberal politics in the context of what can have no politics and enjoins a reconsideration of how the human relates to that. There can be no denying that humanity must understand itself as a species in the face of the Anthropocene, but this species must not be understood to involve an abstract border. It must not be an inside opposed to an outside. It must not assume the possibility of communication or the assimilation of difference.[73] We cannot negotiate with nonlife, with the weird planet, as we would with another human across the proverbial table. We cannot even interact with it. The results of any interaction with it could never be meaningful. These results could not register with the "it" in a way we could understand and therefore would never produce a point of commencement from which to pursue progress. The abdifferent confrontation with the weird planet does not involve the end of history, in which liberalism has triumphed over all to produce an eternally boring sameness, as Lowry fears it might. Nor does it involve the end of nature, the collapse of a space distinguished from humanity that humanity might finally overcome. Nature remains so long as liberal politics remains, even if the weird planet exists as well, if according to altogether different norms. As one commentary on the Anthropocene puts it, albeit in a rather different context, this planet cannot end: "The *planet* does not need to be saved; it existed before organic life, and will go on to exist for some time (probably) well after humans and well after organisms."[74]

Shortly after the "tiny shifting spiral of light" penetrates his body, the Event that most clearly brings Area X into visible and tangible contact with humanity (a monodirectional visibility and tangibility, to be sure), Saul Evans, the lighthouse keeper *cum* Crawler, has a vision:

> The stars no longer shone but flew and scuttled across the sky, and the violence of their passage did not bear scrutiny. He had the sense that something distant had come close from far away, that the stars moved in this way because now they were close enough to be seen as more than tiny points of light.
>
> He was walking toward the lighthouse along the trail, but the moon was hemorrhaging blood into its silver circle, and he knew that terrible things must have happened to the Earth for the moon to be dying, to be about to fall out of the heavens. The oceans were filled with graveyards of trash and every pollutant that had ever been loosed against the natural world. Wars for scant resources had left entire countries nothing but deserts of death and suffering. Disease had spread in its legions and life had begun to mutate into other forms, moaning and mewling in the filthy, burning remnants of once mighty cities, lit by roaring fires that crackled with the smoldering bones of strange, distorted cadavers.[75]

This vision clearly invokes the threat of catastrophic climate change both in its own right and in terms of its effects on political dynamics depending on lines in the dirt and other abstract valorizations to keep score. This globalized death erases political differences rooted in abstract localities. Moreover, just as the official cover story for Area X involves an environmental catastrophe of perhaps human origin and covers up the fact that there is nothing to cover up, no useful knowledge of what is going on with the planet beyond the earth, this passage, in the larger context of the trilogy, suggests the Anthropocene to be a cover-up, a story about the potential loss of human meaning at the hands of an adversary so immense that we stand atop it even as we battle it, the earth itself—a story that obscures a deeper war that is not a war, one being fought between an irreducibly limited humanity and the spatial and temporal scales that not only will always defeat it but also will not even be aware of the war to begin with.

Here we discover the danger of liberalism in this context, as well as the danger of the illiberalism characteristic of Lovecraft's racism, a danger that it poses in addition to the one it poses in the context of politics and society conventionally understood. By dehumanizing those he hated, Lovecraft humanized the Elder Gods and other denizens of the outside. He left open some passage from here to there, and thus left open some means by which to render Thacker's third level of the supernatural in terms of given reality. No superstition, no lack of modernity (real or constructed by those who call themselves modern) protects anyone from the weird planet, and no amount of power to declare borders will forestall the inert force of a nonliving *geos*. The inside and outside such racism defines, like any abstract inside and outside, possess political but not material force (although it may be backed by material force). As Saul walks among the corpses in his vision, he has "the sense that they existed somewhere else, and it was only some hidden pull, like a celestial riptide, that drew them to manifest in that place."[76] These planetary bodies do not exist on earth in a way that allows them to be contained by abstract borders such as the ones distinguishing now from then or here from there. They exist within the weird planet and within a materiality ignorant of the rules by which humans measure themselves and their productions. It exists everywhere and nowhere, everywhen and never. These planetary bodies, abdifferently bordering.

CONCLUSION

LIFE AFTER AFTERMATH

Thus the earth is not dying. But the earth may be turning away from certain forms of existence.

—*Elizabeth Povinelli,*
Geontologies: A Requiem to Late Liberalism

Our lives were rapidly becoming impossible.

—*Jeff VanderMeer,* Borne

As I have suggested throughout this book, Jeff VanderMeer's fiction often features places and spaces we might consider dystopian or post-apocalyptic. The Veniss narrative begins with the former, in a city or region where humans are ruled by the soliminds, and ends as the latter, in a desert wasteland lacking all human-scale reference, lacking all setting. Ambergris rarely calls attention to its dystopian nature, but its lack of government and large-scale institutions, coupled with the eventual revelation that the gray caps have been in charge the whole time, render it implicitly so. The flooded, fungal world of *Finch*—characterized by social and environmental instability, constant fear, and monstrous encounters with nonhuman forces—easily fits into conventional notions of postapocalypse. If Area X fails to be a postapocalyptic landscape, it is only the case because Area X refuses the logic of before and after implicit in the prefix "post-" and obviates any notion of apocalypse. It has always been there, and it refuses all revelation. In each of these creations, VanderMeer has largely focused on the human encounter with dystopia and the postapocalyptic landscape, especially insofar as each presents a challenge to anthropocentric and anthropomorphic knowledge techniques such as critique and history. In each creation, we find nonhuman entities and forces: the meerkats, flesh dogs, and familiars of Veniss; the gray caps of Ambergris; the monsters of Area X and Area X itself. Nonetheless, the focus in each has mainly been on the human and the ways in which it is defeated. What happens to these entities and forces after the human passes away remains unclear and is left to readers' imaginations.

In his most recent fiction, the novel *Borne* (2017) and the related novella *The Strange Bird: A Borne Story* (2017), VanderMeer begins with an already defeated humanity, a ghost that continues to negotiate a dystopian, postapocalyptic landscape even after its life has become impossible.[1] However, he slowly turns his attention to the nonhuman entities and forces poised to inherit the world from the human—entities and forces that do not inherit the world despite its brokenness but precisely because this brokenness has made their lives possible. The world of *Borne* is a world determined by the human, whose various technologies have destroyed pristine nature to the extent that even the memory or myth of such no longer exists. In this world of humanity's creation, individual humans can at best survive. The species can only disappear. This disappearance, however, is not a cause for sadness. Rather, it is only a cause for human sadness. The life that shall inherit the broken places created by humans have their own affects, their own manner of living in the world, outside of the myths and other narratives that humanity tells itself about itself in order to make its own existence meaningful. This final example of fantastic materiality demonstrates what we might call human disappointment, which refers both to the removal of the human from its position as the ruler of the earth as well as to an affect of the nonhuman: the disappointment of ever having been human at all.

For this affect to manifest within the nonhuman, the nonhuman must first live, and to live it must not be, or can no longer be, human. As Rachel, *Borne*'s protagonist and narrator, tells us, in the world of *Borne*, human life is in the process of becoming impossible. This claim is no mere metaphor. Rachel has lived her entire life as a refugee. With her parents, she once fled landmass after landmass as each was swallowed up by rising sea levels; the Westphalian borders these landmasses supported succumbed to the inexorable yet inert materiality of the planet: "I was only six when we left, boarding a ship as refugees. I remember because my parents told me the stories as I grew up. They told me the stories even as we continued to be refugees, moving from camp to camp, country to country, thinking that we could outrun the unraveling of the world. But the world was unraveling in most places."[2] The City, too, is fundamentally broken, ruled in part by a dead or dying Company whose biotechnological creations are left to expire or evolve in a festering pool near its shattered headquarters; a giant flying bear named Mord, a former Company employee transformed into a senseless monster who destroys what he does not control; and the Magician, a genius with biotechnology who transforms the City's children into deadly predators and seeks to return the world to what she idealizes as its previously pristine state.

How any of this came to pass remains unknown. Rachel certainly has no explanation for the City in which she inexplicably lives: "I don't know, it just happened. Everything everywhere collapsed. We didn't try hard enough. We were preyed upon. We had no discipline. We didn't try the right things at the right time. We cared but we didn't do. Too many people, too little space."[3] Whatever the case, Rachel recognizes how her life must change, how even the small place she and her partner, Wick, have carved out for themselves will inevitably be swept away:

Every day brought us closer to a point where we would have to redefine our relationship to the Balcony Cliffs, and to each other. And, in the middle of all routes, my apartment, where, pulled taught by our connections, we fucked, we screwed, we made love, equidistant from any border that might encroach, any enemy that might try to enter. We could be greedy there

and selfish there, and there we saw each other fully. Or at least
thought we did, because whatever we had, it was the enemy of
the world outside.[4]

For all of the mistakes she makes in *Borne*, about her place in the world
and about the world itself, Rachel is correct here in ways she does not yet
and cannot yet understand. If she and Wick, within the Balcony Cliffs,
are "equidistant from any border that might encroach," it is not because
these borders are far away, either outside of or at the boundary of the
Balcony Cliffs. Rather, these borders are everywhere at once. Life has
become impossible not because this or that place is broken, but because
for the human all places have become broken. As Povinelli tells us, the
planet does not support every form of existence forever.

Given such passages as these, and given the political context in
which it was published, it would be difficult for any reader not to see
Borne as a partisan statement about the need for political action on climate change and the other ravages of the Anthropocene, one even more
pressing than the one made by the Southern Reach trilogy, which was
published when the prospect of fighting such forces seemed at the very
least possible, if not actually likely. *Borne* was released in the first months
of the Trump administration, which has pulled the United States out
of the Paris climate agreement of 2016 and whose Environmental
Protection Agency head not only denies climate science but seems to
actively despise the environment.[5] It was written during a period when
the governor of VanderMeer's home state of Florida, Rick Scott, forbade
the use of the term "climate change" by employees of his Department
of Environmental Protection (despite the clear dangers Florida specifically faces from climate change).[6] In this context, *Borne* indeed makes a
powerful statement about the damage humanity has done to the material
earth itself as well as to the possibility of politics on the surface of the
earth. *Borne*'s partisanship most clearly becomes visible insofar as it represents the impossibility of political life—of living according to abstractions called "borders" or "nations" that the planet refuses to acknowledge
or respect—under the threat of climate change.

Without such abstractions, however, human life may well become impossible. Later in *Borne*, the war among the Company, Mord, and the Magician finally penetrates the home Rachel had made with Wick, causing her to once again flee an abstractly defined space of impermanent safety and venture out into the materiality of the planet. As she puts it, in what seems to be both a testament to human resilience and a recognition that mere survival is all that remains to the human: "We had lost the Balcony Cliffs. We had given up our temporary shelter. We'd lost the city proper. And now we were about to lose the surface. Apparently we'd been richer than we thought, to suffer such continual diminishment and still be alive."[7] Steven Shaviro writes, "There is no triumphalism in [Rachel]; she is not any sort of savior. Surviving itself is the most that she can hope for; but survival always has its price, since the more you survive the more you suffer."[8] Rachel's suffering does not derive from any existential dilemma. That she is merely surviving suggests that she has moved beyond lack, beyond an existence that seeks more and that demands meaning. Her diminishment has nothing to do with her brute life but with her humanity and with what makes her life worth living in human terms. However, this loss, which Rachel generally accepts without despair, does not imply the loss of life as such. In fact, it makes possible the continuance of life as such beyond the human—a deeper, planetary survival.

VanderMeer refers to this surviving life, what lives on after another form of existence passes, as "life in the broken places." In an interview about *Borne*, VanderMeer describes his impetus for writing it:

> Then I thought about the idea of what I would call "life in the broken places," because there are places that are even quite urbanized or industrialized that have more biodiversity than you might think. Once I had this ruined city and this Company, I thought, What lives in the cracks of this place, and how might it have agency?
>
> There's a story in the backdrop of biotech and little creatures—that have their own stories that come to the fore towards the end of the book.[9]

Similarly, in the closing moments of the video trailer for *Borne*, VanderMeer describes the novel's engagement with the relation between life and its material condition: "The difference in *Borne*, is it's not talking about pristine wilderness, it's talking about life in the broken places, life in the places where there is contamination, but it's still worth preserving."[10] This life, which in VanderMeer's narration to the trailer appears as a duck with a broken wing and other nonhuman forms, stands on material conditions, namely an urbanized landscape characterized by pollution and waste, which humans may have had a hand in shaping. However, this condition, despite its relationship to the human, has increasingly become for these nonhuman forms of life rather than for the one humanity insists on as the measure of all things. Just as Area X suggests a new definition of geopolitics, *Borne*'s City and earth suggest a new form of partisanship, one in which material conditions take sides over the issue of what form of life shall flourish.

This partisanship has nothing to do with conscious choice; nor does it suggest the possibility of reasoned, democratic debate. Materiality cannot be argued with, and it does not respect the logic of "one person, one vote." It cannot be reached by these human techniques. It is not simply an actor in a political drama. It is also the stage on which that drama takes place, what can end the drama by fiat. Because it is both actor and stage, the materiality VanderMeer calls the broken places can never be neutral, and its nonneutrality, its partisanship, can never take an anthropocentric stance. It is only for itself, the relationship it once enjoyed with the human either never having been what the human thought it was or now eroding as new relationships with new forms of life manifest. The question of the preservation of life here has nothing to do with meaning, with what will be lost if human civilization ends, or even with the falseness of human meaning in the face of cosmic indifference. The broken places, which continue to be breaking places, engender new forms of life. These forms are not human, and they care not at all for politics anthropocentrically or anthropomorphically conceived.

VanderMeer deploys this idea of "life in the broken places" in the companion novella to *Borne*, where a recently liberated piece of biotech that knows itself only as the Strange Bird encounters other pieces of biotech whose liberation preexists her own and has achieved the status of a new, autonomous form of nature that has manifested where pristine nature can no longer exist (the question of whether it ever existed being a child's question, as the psychologist would tell us): "They were the creatures from the broken places. They were the insurgents that no one could see." Borne, the autonomous piece of biotech that gives this world its name, also encounters these creatures and gives them a name of their own, which he discusses with Rachel. She states:

> Borne coined the term *Nocturnalia*, for the way that life now
> welled up in unexpected ways whenever darkness slid over the
> city. There had always been a life out there in the blackness
> that did not include us and that moved to its own rhythm. But
> added to that now, what made the night both opportunistic
> and perilous, were the others lurking, so many out in it,
> thinking the night gave them cover. We couldn't interpret
> these others, hardly knew where they had come from, could
> not grasp, either, their allegiances, or the eruption of those who
> worshiped Mord in the aftermath of the Magician's failure,
> who sided with the great bear and chose to give their fealty and
> foolishly thought this made them immune.[11]

By the end of *Borne*, Rachel will come to understand that the Nocturnalia will inherit the earth—in fact had already inherited the earth, although "inherit" implies an ownership and a set of values that have long since outlived their utility. Her time and the time of humanity have passed, and nothing of that time—neither the material conditions it produced nor the values according to which this production took place—will last. After Borne leaves her to dwell in the City with the Nocturnalia, Rachel wanders in search of him, a self-professed ghost among the ruins:

> As the ghost immersed herself in the night, became steeped
> in it and more comfortable, the ghost's search became more
> and more meaningless. The ghost's purpose changed and the
> ghost became a chronicler in her head of a damaged city, a

city that could not go on like this forever, torn between foes and monsters, before it, too, became a ghost. The body still gasped and drew breath and reanimated itself—contained the capacity to be rejuvenated, even now. But not forever. Eventually the collective memory would fail, and travelers, if travelers ever came again, would find a stretch of desert that had once been a vast ocean and hardly a sign that a city had ever been here.[12]

In the world of *Borne*, a ghost is what lives despite its place being broken and what continues to exist even as its place breaks. A ghost experiences its place turning away from it because such turning is part and parcel of materiality's inert inexorability. A ghost is a life in the broken places that is broken by these places—what perhaps broke these places and itself at the same time. A ghost is a being of mere survival, of subsistence. It can no longer rely on history for its meaning because history is over; nor can it retreat into nature because nature is now for something else. A ghost is a planetary body, what the weird planet relates to and, in so relating, destroys. But for all a ghost is, there are crucial things it is not. A ghost is neither supernatural nor metaphysical. A ghost is not a spirit of something else; it is not what has passed but now returns; nor does it signify a contradictory mode of existence characterized by crossing the border that separates life and death. Most importantly, a ghost is not a last thing.

At the conclusion of *Borne*, Rachel, like the rest of humanity, has become a ghost and has reached her end. However, there is more to the conclusion to the novel than this end. For *Borne*'s fantastic materiality, this end can only constitute an ending that does not imply a beginning from scratch in a new world; rather, this ending indicates a continuation through the remains of the old (a world that will not, however, be old for what continues). I will turn my attention momentarily to this continuation. For now, the nature of this ending, the end of the human that is in no way the end of the planet, is worth considering insofar as it represents a triumph of the new weird over the logics of the genres with which it so often interacts: fantasy, science fiction, and horror.

If we understand these three genres to reflect three aspects of modern human thought—the desire for a return to the past before the world became corrupted by the change wrought by modernity, the desire for a future produced by modern means that is different than the past or present, and the fear that modernity itself and the progress it espouses have only ever been lies—then we might see the new weird as at best merely rearranging furniture. If the new weird is an attempt to hybridize three aspects of modern human thought, then it has always been an endeavor whose success was compromised a priori by the tools with which it was forced to work. However, far from hybridizing fantasy, science fiction, and horror, *Borne* does away with all three subgenres of fantastika by way of the ends of its three primary antagonists. By the conclusion of the novel, the Magician—whose very name suggests a belief in magic and whose plans for the City appear to Rachel as "an enticing snow globe of a scene by a mighty river, with docks and piers and a dazzling sky with birds in mid-flight amid the first signs of spring and bright, modern buildings on the land beyond that had never suffered war. A scene that would fill anyone from our ruined city with such yearnings and, perhaps, recognition"—will be dead.[13] The last vestiges of the Company, whose technologies promised the future but destroyed it instead, will be in ruins. Mord—a composite of the monster from nature (a bear), the monster from within (a bear produced from a human subject), the monster from the past (the last revenge of science and capitalism), and, most of all, the created monster—will likewise be dead. The regressive longing of fantasy, the progressive thrust of science fiction, and the aggressive despair of horror will not survive.

This liquidation of genre and the modes of thought each represents takes place on more than a symbolic level. Through the fantastic materiality of VanderMeer's "life in the broken places," *Borne* overcomes the limitations that each genre places on ending itself. These limitations require every narrative to be human and concern itself only with human meaning (or its lack). For fantasy, the human once possessed an essential meaning that was lost with the Fall. All subsequent existence therefore involves a desire for healing or return, the final stage of Clute's grammar of fantasy. Clute defines healing as "what occurs after the worst has been experienced and defeated. It is the greening of the Waste Land or the recovery from Amnesia on the part of the Hero or the escape from Bondage and the Metamorphosis into the desired shape and fullness of those who have been wounded/imprisoned by the Dark Lord."[14] By contrast, science fiction involves a forward movement, a progress through history according to which human meaning might be achieved in the future by way of the discovery of the truths of material world. Clute names the final stage of the grammar of science fiction "topia," which may take the form of utopia or dystopia, depending on the point of view of those who experience it. It is "the Jerusalem whose gates have opened by conceptual breakthrough for those who have won through: it is a *place* where life is going to be led in accordance with the truths discovered."[15] In such a place, history has ended and human meaning has been achieved finally.

In *Borne*, clearly there can be no return. The environment cannot be reset to a pristine state. The political order cannot be reestablished. Moreover, should it become possible to do either thing, nothing would be fixed. Modern politics and related techniques would almost certainly reproduce the same crises that led to the conditions we find in *Borne* at the start. True return cannot be the renewal of the modern but the anti-Fall, a reemergence of the state of the world radically prior to modernity. And just as there can be no return, there can be no arrival in any utopia or dystopia. The world is too broken to support the perfectly operational nation or any other human institution. The rules that would govern such a place can never be understood finally; they always elude the human because the human produces them as an ideal in the first place. Materiality will never conform to our expectations for it.

The impossibility of both return and arrival should be cause for pessimism, and often is insofar as the only option that seems left to us when fantasy and science fiction fail is horror. In horror, the narrative threads that bind the human to its world and the events of that world to one another unravel, exposing the human to at best the uncanny and homelessness and at worst the cosmic indifference of the Elder Gods and the brute materiality they embody. For Clute, the grammar of horror ends in aftermath, when the human becomes aware "that the Story is done. This moment . . . prefigures a world incapable of change."[16] Aftermath, by denying narrative and the meaning-making techniques thereof, denies both progression to a new, produced meaning and regression to an old, essential one. It thus stands opposed to structural conclusions of science fiction and fantasy: the arrival in topia and the return to Eden. Clute further articulates horror's opposition to meaning as follows: "the end of Story [i.e., 'topia' or 'return'] constitutes an [sic] pastoral arrival in Eden: there is no Story to tell because there is no problem. But Aftermath is all problem, like muskeg: problem without solution, a geography without watershed."[17] Aftermath demonstrates the impossibility of meaning, the mendacity of history, the hypocrisy of critique, and the delusion of humanity's self-regard. Of course, horror can only represent the end of all narrative in narrative form. Just as for Jameson the utopia as a form more often than not becomes a meditation on the impossibility of utopia rather than an actual representation of it, horror at its best can only demonstrate the impossibility of representing a truly inhuman condition.[18] Horror endeavors to produce a final act of critique with regard to anthropocentric and anthropomorphic knowledge practices; it endeavors to demonstrate that these practices are not capable of representing the truth of the world: in face of the abyss, the monster, materiality, the cosmos, and so on, the human is nothing.

Even more problematically, the insistence that the human is nothing keeps the focus of horror precisely on the human. As I have discussed, the subject of horror is all too often the modern human, commonly represented, especially in the nineteenth-century gothic and Lovecraft's weird, as a white male scientist or other professional—a rational actor who believes less in the supernatural than he does in, for example, the powers of empiricism to reveal fundamental truths or the powers of the invisible hand to balance accounts and produce the social good. When these fictions are revealed as fictions, the subject of horror loses everything. To translate this line of argument into Clute's language, in aftermath, the subject of horror retains a capacity to identify problem but loses any capacity for solution. Without solution, there can be no progress, but Clute's formulation seems to forget that the same can be said for problem. It may be the case that the problem–solution pair drive history as well as the production of human meaning and values.

However, the suggestion that the loss of half of the pair is itself a problem, a truly objective problem, remains thoroughly anthropocentric. Lack of solution is only a problem for the human, for whom the problem–solution pair articulates a manner of knowing and a set of values that materiality does not recognize as its own. Whatever loss we find in aftermath, which refers to a state of mind rather than to the material conditions of the planet, remains a human loss, one that should be comic insofar as it shows the human to lack meaning but becomes nearly tragic when we come to understand the degree to which this loss only verifies to the human all that it once possessed. The Veniss milieu narrativizes this loss by way of "The City," in which characters struggle to arrive in a place that may never have existed in the name of the familiar. Ambergris does so by way of Mary Sabon's resistance to the material world confronting her at every turn—a resistance that finally crumbles when that materiality rises from the underworld and renders human life simultaneously impossible and worth fighting for. Area X does so by way of the confrontation between the Southern Reach and an adversary that takes on no human dimension and that cannot provide any human-readable feedback. This is a confrontation that in the end fails to even be a confrontation, and thus provides for the human no recognition of its humanity whatsoever. Even as these creations disappoint the human, they tend to remain focused on the human and all that this disappointment means to it.

Borne and *The Strange Bird*, as a single narrative of human loss and inhuman inheritance, do something else altogether. This something else begins with Rachel's discovery of a bit of biotech she salvages from the fur of the giant bear, Mord. She takes it home and names it Borne, at which point she begins to think of it as a "him." Much of the novel that follows describes Rachel's attempts to raise Borne and the degree to which Borne's inhumanity, which drives him to consume nearly all of the life he encounters without ever producing any waste of his own, renders impossible Rachel's attempts to humanize him. Among other things, Rachel teaches Borne about her past and all that she has lost. When she recalls Borne's question about how she knows this past had in fact happened, she thinks to herself: "Because of its absence now, because I still felt the loss of it but I didn't know how to convey that to Borne then, because he had never lost anything. Not back then. He just kept accumulating, sampling, tasting. He kept gaining parts of the world, while I kept losing them."[19] In response to this and similar narratives about human knowledge and affect, Borne decides to fight Mord and free the City of his capricious yet endless destruction.

Before he engages with the giant bear, Borne tells Rachel of his goals: "I know how to make everything right again. I can see it so clearly, and I can do it now. . . . And in the end everything will be okay again between us and you can live in the Balcony Cliffs and I'll move back in with you and it'll be like the times we ran down the corridors laughing. . . . It'll be just like that."[20] Borne does in fact destroy Mord, but he destroys himself in the process. As Rachel puts it, as she watches two giant monsters battle each other over the ruins of the City, Mord, as a monster, is the better of the two: "[Borne] would not win. He would not win. Weapon he may be, but Borne was not, in the end, hardened as Mord was hardened."[21] If Borne lacks the monstrous hardness necessary to fight and defeat Mord, such is the case because he possesses a tiny amount of something else, something from which the planet has turned away in this age of giant monsters: humanity. Rachel recalls that once Borne had asked her if he was a weapon. She tells him that he is a person, "But like a person, you can be a weapon too."[22] Perhaps Borne can be many things, but in having borne Borne, in having raised him, Rachel gave his life purpose and meaning, and thus corrupted what would have allowed him to survive in this world: his monstrosity, his "itness," his "being weapon." His death is a poignant moment, but the affect it involves, loss and sadness, remains human. Rachel loses her child, who gives his life to save hers and provide her, and a doomed humanity, with few more moments of survival. After Mord's death, after the end of the Company, and after Rachel kills the Magician, new life appears in the City, "like Bornes that want nothing from the old world" because "they need nothing from it."[23] Monsters inherit the earth, but only by way of a humanized one whose life takes on meaning by creating the conditions of this inheritance.

This is not, however, the end of the story. In *The Strange Bird*, the eponymous piece of biotech flees the lab in which she was created as it falls to nebulous forces. She finds herself flying through an open sky, driven by an internal compass she can neither understand nor resist. Sanji, the Strange Bird's creator, describes the compass as follows: "The compass is the heart of you. The compass is at the heart of you. I've hidden it deep, and whatever else you give up, you must never give this up." When the Strange Bird winds up in the hands of the Magician, she is forced to give up everything else. The Magician dismantles her to the core of her very being: "And still this could not describe the agony as the Magician took her wings from her, broke her spine, removed her bones one by one, but left her alive, writhing and formless on the stone table, still able to see, and thus watching as the Magician casually threw away so many parts that were irreplaceable. As she gasped through a slit of a mouth, her beak removed as well."

After spending years as the Magician's living cloak, the Strange Bird is recovered by Wick and Rachel, who transform it into several, smaller Strange Birds, each driven by the one thing the Strange Bird never gave up: her compass. The birds set out to find where the compass compels them to go. One survives the journey to "a ruined laboratory station, an apple tree growing beside it. Twin to the lab from which she had escaped." There the remnant of the Strange Bird finds "a mirror reflection of her old self, the bird of many colors, the iridescent splendor of it all. The old her, the beautiful her, the one with no experience." This twin conveys to the Strange Bird, and the spirit of her creator, that the world is broken and that she, Sanji's lover, wishes that it could be otherwise. The Strange Bird replies with Sanji's words: *"I could not be with you, my love. But I can watch over you all my days."* Here is where *The Strange Bird* becomes truly weird. Just as Borne's death proves affective, so is this reunion steeped in pathos. However, this pathos, unlike that of *Borne* (which is also felt by Rachel), is only for the reader. The Strange Bird feels something too, but that something is not human. When Borne tells Rachel that he will save the world, she sees in him "the false power of remorse, which makes you think that by the strength of your convictions, your emotions, you can make everything right even when you can't. Remorse and a false vision made Borne say crazy things, I thought."[24]

The Strange Bird sees not only the falseness of the powers of remorse but also the falseness of falseness. That is, she understands that even the negation of remorse remains itself a human affect. The sadness the Strange Bird feels at the end of her story is not for any human to feel; nor does it refer to a humanity now absent from the world. Her sadness comes from the knowledge that she never should have involved herself with humanity to begin with. When the compulsion that had guided her throughout her quest turns out to be merely human, she understands that it means nothing to her. In response to this recognition, she all at once grasps the importance of making nests and finding shelter against the cliffs she will now call home with her companion precisely because these are not human things. "Everyone who had created the Strange Bird or interfered with her or had hopes or fears that had been placed in her, or wished her ill, was dead." As such, "all the senseless things. All the senseless and unimportant things that fell away from the Strange Bird in that moment, that were forgotten or became meaningless. It had been a human need, the compass pulsing at her heart. And she was, in the end, much diminished for having followed it." There is no renewal here, only novelty. Human goals, motivations, desires, processes, techniques, narratives, meanings, histories, lives, environments—they pass and will not return. Nothing returns. Nonetheless, something always comes, but this coming does not mean anything. It involves no progress and no solution because nothing is broken for what comes. That is what life after aftermath is.

Borne, and especially *The Strange Bird*, are about life after aftermath. They do not seek to tell a human story about what living in aftermath looks like, or about the challenges of remaining human biologically, ontologically, epistemologically, politically, aesthetically, or ethically. They are not *The Road Warrior* (1981) or *28 Days Later* (2002) or *Children of Men* (2006). Rather, they tell the story of what happens after aftermath, after the loss of solution no longer poses a problem because the form of life for whom such a loss represents a problem has become impossible. They tell a story about materiality turning away from this form of life to present opportunities for new forms of life to arise in the broken places, which are no longer broken but are whole places, the condition of this new life. Insofar as it does not include the human, for which anything outside of itself can never live up to the standards it creates, such a materiality can only ever be fantastic: an uncritical, ahistoricist, and meaningless fiction. VanderMeer teaches us that even if the production of such fictions will not save us, they may show us the planet saving itself.

AFTERWORD

JEFF VANDERMEER

For as long as I can remember, I have been interested in the irrationality of the human mind and the complexity of natural systems, including the beauty and strangeness of creatures that we might think of as falling under the umbrella of "weird biology." Investigations of what it means to be human, living on a planet alive with organisms we still don't fully understand, whose life cycles and senses are often so different from our own, fill me with awe and have always informed my writing. In many cases, those life cycles and the attempt to imagine what it might be like to experience the life of another species has even affected the structure of my novels and stories.

I was drawn to formal experimentalism early in my career in part for that reason: wanting to find the structures and narratological approaches that would allow me to get beyond some of the foundational assumptions we have about nature and culture. I moved away from that kind of visible experiment in the Southern Reach novels because I became fascinated by the idea of hidden patterns and invisible experiments that would be perhaps even more effective because they would registered, for the most part, more subconsciously and thus have even more impact. From the late 1980s, too, my stories and novels have often grappled with climate change and ecological devastation, and part of this engagement has taken the form of thinking about the rate of the strange versus the familiar in fiction—which simply means that I think of some of my stories as renovations and some as attempted innovation. Others are renovations that started out as innovations but collapsed inward because the weight of the strange could not be supported by the scaffolding I had chosen.

Given all of this, it is perhaps no surprise—especially considering I have sent up academic writing in works like "The Early History of Ambergris"—that I fall into the category of being fascinated by literary criticism but also wary of easy interpretation. The author may be dead, but the author knows sometimes that, for example, something seen as symbolic is just a bit of stage business, or the detail that reviewers overlook is indeed important thematically. Someone once interpreted a rose in a lapel in "The Strange Case of X," a story mentioned in this book, in terms of the medieval symbolism of a rose, when in fact I had put it there so readers could identify a character later in the story. The medieval symbolism of the rose, in addition to being irrelevant to the story, obliterated a genuine reading of the actual, intended symbolism of certain other elements. I understand that literary criticism is not for the author, but at the same time the author cannot be faulted for rebelling against a clear misreading.

Especially when writing fiction that often deals with the environment and animals, I have grown weary, too, of some people's foundational assumptions about these topics, as superimposed over my work. Animal behavior science has advanced well beyond book culture and popular culture's ability to keep up, apparently. I am also wary of mapping literature in terms of rigid ideological positions because no matter how much I might sympathize with some of those positions, fiction itself is a living, breathing organism that can be both contrary in its habits and behavior, and complex enough to contain many opposing ideas. In short, fiction is not a thesis but a journey or a conversation, and rigid ideological interpretations of my work are a bit like applying an egg slicer to a cuttlefish: not useful to anyone.

In that context, I was happy to read *None of This Is Normal*, because Ben Robertson has found ways to talk about my fiction that doesn't reduce it down to just one thing and provides vivid analysis that feels accurate, inasmuch as literary criticism can be objective. I welcome opposing views of any piece of fiction or body of work and value honest negative reviews where it is clear the critic got what I was up to and just found it lacking. Indeed, I appreciate that—it's a kind of service to the author. But the worst kind of literary criticism, or reviewing for that matter, is the positive or glowing analysis that in the end seriously misunderstands the work. And I don't feel either in my head or my heart that the author has misunderstood me. Instead, I find much here that fascinates me.

One of the values of interesting literary criticism for the author is this sense of being understood—which is in a sense the idea of being vindicated, especially for someone like me whose work started out in the small press and rose slowly through the ranks. You have to develop a thick skin and take the long view; you have to believe that in the end you will find your audience and you will be better understood. Even in terms of issues like "was the new weird a movement or a moment?," the author takes an even-handed approach, with the original discussion almost seventeen years ago long since subsumed by a lacerating welter of interpretations and misinterpretations.

Beyond this value, which of course is not the point of literary criticism, is the sense of discovery. In reading *None of This Is Normal*, I jotted down notes at several points and experienced the excitement of encountering books and ideas that I was either unaware of or had only a cursory knowledge of. In a sense, reading Robertson's book completed the debrief for series like the Southern Reach. What I mean by debrief is that after the publication cycle for a book of mine and for a series, I go back and I analyze the reactions to pull out associations, influences, and ideas that I did not consider part of my conscious intent. I research these associations, influences, and ideas. At the end of this process, I sometimes I discover the reviewer or critic was spot on, and I just didn't realize it when writing the book. Most of the time, it simply adds another sedimentary layer of knowledge—philosophy, science, etc.—for the next thing I write.

What this means is that as much as *None of This Is Normal* engages with my work and seeks to explicate it, I will now use what I've learned from *None of This Is Normal* as inspiration for future fiction. It will contaminate my narratives directly and indirectly, and I will internalize this contamination as idea broken down and then built up again as image, as character, as landscape, and as storytelling.

For all of this, and for a thoughtful and complex reading, I am grateful.

ACKNOWLEDGMENTS

There is, at least, one norm that is not a construction, namely the one that insists that every book comes about through the generosity of others.

I could not have known in 2012, when Paul Youngquist asked me if I had ever read this book *Finch* by Jeff VanderMeer, that I would eventually write so much about it. So I thank Paul for the suggestion and for numerous subsequent conversations, as well as the Corner Bar in Boulder where these conversations took place. Other colleagues at the University of Colorado have contributed to my specific thinking here and to my thinking in general, including Adam Bradley, Thora Brylowe, Jeff Cox, Jeremy Green, Ali Hassan, Cheryl Higashida, Janice Ho, Kelly Hurley, Stephen Graham Jones, William Kuskin, Jill Heydt-Stevenson, John Stevenson, Eric White, Maria Windell, Laura Winkiel, and Sue Zemka. Thanks to all of them for this and more. Among my colleagues, I wish to single out Jason Gladstone, whose intelligence and insight shaped this project in ways I shall never fully be able to appreciate. And here I also want to mention the beer list at Backcountry Pizza, over which this intelligence and insight were routinely on display.

Beyond Boulder, I have benefited from long and brief conversations with a great number of scholars of genre, media theory, and literature. Chief among my interlocutors are Gerry Canavan and Timothy Murphy, who have offered not only helpful advice about my writing and thinking but also on the profession and this project's place within it. Thanks to

Rebekah Sheldon for friendship and her capacity to make difficult thinking look easy. Thanks to Darren Wershler for his comments on the proposal for this project. Thanks to numerous others at the International Conference on the Fantastic in the Arts and the Science Fiction Research Association conferences where some of the ideas for this book were first discussed, including Brian Attebery, Ritch Calvin, A. P. Canavan, Dan Creed, Neil Easterbrook, Andrew Ferguson, Paweł Frelik, Dan Hassler-Forest, Kate Hayles, David Higgins, the late Michael Levy, Sean Matheroo, Peter Melville, Hugh O'Connell, John Rieder, Valérie Savard, Mark Scroggins, and Derek Theiss. You are my people.

Thanks to Barbara Cole, Jason Embry, Joe Genovese, Gordon Hadfield, Alissa Jones, and Sasha Steensen. They know why.

Thanks to those teachers who have shaped my thought and kindled in me a desire to know more: Fawzia Afzal-Khan, the late Paul Arthur, Bruce Bidwell, Jim Bono, Joseph Conte, Janet Cutler, Robert Daly, Elizabeth Grosz, Dave Hicks, David Schmid, Art Simon, and Tim Watson.

Thanks to Steven Shaviro, whose comments greatly encouraged me even as they illuminated aspects of my project I had not yet fully understood. Thanks also to Jason Weidemann for all of his help, and especially for crazy schemes.

Finally, thanks and love to my family, who might not understand what this is or why I have done it, but who have supported me on what must seem like my abnormal endeavors for more than four decades now. More than thanks and love (there are no words) to Beep (RIP), Chip (RIP), Ajax (RIP), Java, Ada, and Sheena, who sat on my lap, played with me, and took me for walks when work became too much. All that and more to Lori, the material condition of my life, that without which I could not do this, could not be me.

NOTES

INTRODUCTION

1.   Weird fiction is mainly associated with the work of certain writers—such as Algernon Blackwood, H. P. Lovecraft, and Clark Ashton Smith—from the late nineteenth and early twentieth centuries. Writers associated with the two main periods of new weird fiction include Ramsey Campbell, Clive Barker, and Thomas Ligotti on the one hand, and on the other VanderMeer, China Miéville, Steph Swainston, and K. J. Bishop. Some of these writers (especially Lovecraft and Miéville) have enjoyed massive critical attention, as have the weird and new weird more generally. The best introductions to weird and new weird fiction can be found in collections edited by Jeff VanderMeer and Ann VanderMeer: *The Weird: A Compendium of Strange and Dark Stories* (New York: Tor Books, 2012) and *The New Weird* (San Francisco, Calif.: Tachyon Publications, 2008). For a fuller discussion of these genres, their periodizations, and the use to which they have been put by scholars, see chapter 1.

2.   See Siobhan Carroll, "The Terror and the Terroir: The Ecological Uncanny in New Weird Exploration Narratives," *Paradoxa* 28 (2016): 67–89; and Alison Sperling, "Second Skins: A Body-Ecology of Jeff VanderMeer's The Southern Reach Trilogy," *Paradoxa* 28 (2016): 214–38. These essays focus exclusively on the Southern Reach trilogy. Not only has little scholarly attention been paid to this important work but also none has been paid to what precedes it. However, the number of conference papers I have heard and heard of on VanderMeer—at the International Conference on the Fantastic in the Arts, the Science Fiction Research Association, and elsewhere—as well as a general sense I get from other academics in genre studies, postwar studies, the environmental humanities, and speculative realism in its many forms

suggests that he is one of the next big things, and thus an amelioration of this situation may be in the offing.

1. AMBERGRIS RULES

1. Jeff VanderMeer, *Finch* (Portland, Ore.: Underland Press, 2009), 3.

2. VanderMeer, *Finch*, 6.

3. VanderMeer, *Finch*, 7.

4. VanderMeer, *Finch*, 29.

5. Ann VanderMeer's work as an editor, on its own as well as in collaboration with Jeff VanderMeer, deserves scholarly attention for its own sake. There can be no doubt that she has been responsible for guiding into print, and into the public consciousness, some of the most important texts, writers, and trends in recent genre fiction. As with Jeff VanderMeer's own history as an editor— and much else of interest in this context no doubt—I must leave this topic aside as outside the scope of this book. Summary bibliographies of both Jeff VanderMeer and Ann VanderMeer's are available at the Internet Speculative Fiction Database, http://www.isfdb.org.

6. The following short essay offers a succinct introduction to the concept: Paul Crutzen, "Geology of Mankind," *Nature* 415 (2002): 23. For a longer discussion of the origins of the term and its utility, see W. Steffen et al., "The Anthropocene: Conceptual and Historical Perspectives," *Philosophical Transactions of the Royal Society A: Mathematical, Physical and Engineering Sciences* 369, no. 1938 (2011): 842–67. The designation of the current geologic epoch as the Anthropocene has yet to be formerly adopted by major professional bodies of geologists, although a formal request for such designation has been submitted to the International Geological Congress by its Working Group on the Anthropocene. See Damian Carrington, "The Anthropocene Epoch: Scientists Declare Dawn of Human-Influenced Age," *Guardian*, August 29, 2016, https://www.theguardian.com. The Holocene coincides with the period of human history, which comprises roughly the last 10,000 years.

7. Jan Zalasiewicz argues that these fossils themselves will be insignificant in the context of geological time. Zalasiewicz, *The Earth after Us: What Legacy Will Humans Leave in the Rocks?* (Oxford: Oxford University Press, 2009).

8. Joshua Rothman, "The Weird Thoreau," *New Yorker,* January 14, 2015, http://www.newyorker.com.

9. See Jeff VanderMeer, "Hauntings in the Anthropocene: An Initial Exploration," Environmental Critique, July 16, 2016, https://environmentalcritique.wordpress.com; and Andrew Hageman, "The Sick One-Sentence Joke Version of the Last 12,000 Years: A Conversation between Timothy Morton and Jeff VanderMeer," *Paradoxa* 28 (2016): 41–65.

10. For discussions of this outstripping, see Timothy Clark, "Scale: Derangements of Scale," in *Telemorphosis: Theory in the Era of Climate Change,* ed. Tom Cohen, 148–66 (Ann Arbor, Mich.: Open Humanities Press, 2012); and Derek Woods, "Scale Critique for the Anthropocene," *Minnesota Review* 2014, no. 83 (2014): 133–42.

11. Francis Fukuyama, *The End of History and the Last Man* (New York: Free Press, 2006), xii. The 2006 book-length version of this argument, from which I quote here, builds on an earlier essay: Fukuyama, "The End of History?," *National Interest* 16 (1989): 3–18.

12. Fukuyama, "End of History?," 4.

13. Bill McKibben, *The End of Nature* (New York: Anchor Books, 1989), 8.

14. Dipesh Chakrabarty, "Postcolonial Studies and the Challenge of Climate Change," *New Literary History* 43, no. 1 (2012): 9.

15. Marx famously deploys the term in the section on "Estranged Labor" in *Economic and Philosophic Manuscripts of 1844,* ed. Duncan J. Struik, trans. Martin Milligan, 106–19 (New York: International Publishers, 1993). This relatively humanistic Marx, who was as yet a disciple of Hegel and Feuerbach, provides an object of critique for Louis Althusser in *For Marx,* trans. Ben Brewster (London: Verso, 1990), 43–48.

16. Timothy Clark, "What on World Is the Earth? The Anthropocene and Fictions of the World," *Oxford Literary Review* 35, no. 1 (2013): 9.

17. Clark, "What on World Is the Earth?," 14.

18. Amitav Ghosh notes the way in which the Anthropocene defeats the literary given called "setting," which involves—in its modern, mimetic forms at any rate—human-scaled periods of time and parcels of space. See Ghosh, *The Great Derangement: Climate Change and the Unthinkable* (Chicago: University of Chicago Press, 2016), 58–63. I discuss Ghosh's understanding of setting and the limits it imposes on fiction in chapter 2.

19. Bruno Latour, "Agency at the Time of the Anthropocene," in *New Literary History* 45, no. 1 (2014): 1. Note that by the term "modernism" Latour refers to modernity and its characteristic modes of thought rather than the constellation of early twentieth-century artistic, literary, cultural, and philosophical movements in Europe and the United States. For Latour's discussion of modernism, see *We Have Never Been Modern* (Cambridge, Mass.: Harvard University Press, 1993).

20. Donna J. Haraway, *Staying with the Trouble: Making Kin in the Chthulucene* (Durham, N.C.: Duke University Press, 2016), 2.

21. McKenzie Wark, *Molecular Red: Theory for the Anthropocene* (London: Verso, 2015), 218.

22. Apart from its capacity to name an historical period characterized by human knowledge of the conjunction of history and nature, and of the cataclysm this conjunction is producing, the Anthropocene has come define a period in Euro-American academic thought. A veritable cottage industry devoted to understanding and describing the Anthropocene has sprung up in recent years. It is thus impossible to offer a bibliography of relevant texts. In addition to those I have discussed here, useful discussions of the Anthropocene for humanities scholars include: Jedediah Purdy, *After Nature: A Politics for the Anthropocene* (Cambridge, Mass.: Harvard University Press, 2015); Cohen, *Telemorphosis*; Jeremy Davies, *The Birth of the Anthropocene* (Berkeley: University of California Press, 2016); John Robert McNeill and Peter Engelke, *The Great Acceleration: An Environmental History of the Anthropocene since 1945* (Cambridge, Mass.: Harvard University Press, 2014); and Christophe Bonneuil and Jean-Baptiste Fressoz, *The Shock of the Anthropocene: The Earth, History, and Us* (London: Verso, 2016). For discussions of writing and other artistic practices in the Anthropocene, see Stacy Alaimo, *Exposed: Environmental Politics and Pleasures in Posthuman Times* (Minneapolis: University of Minnesota Press, 2016); and the essays collected in a special issue on "Writing the Anthropocene," edited by Kate Marshall and Tobias Boes, *Minnesota Review*, no. 83 (2014).

23. Ann VanderMeer and Jeff VanderMeer, eds., *The New Weird* (San Francisco, Calif.: Tachyon Publications, 2008), 317. VanderMeer and VanderMeer collect some of the most important participants and statements in this

lengthy debate. For the full debate, see Kathryn Cramer, "The New Weird Archives," Kathryn Cramer, July 23, 2007, http://www.kathryncramer.com/kathryn_cramer/2007/07/the-new-weird-a.html.

24. VanderMeer and VanderMeer, *New Weird*, 318.

25. VanderMeer and VanderMeer, *New Weird*, 319.

26. Jeff VanderMeer, *Why Should I Cut Your Throat? Excursions into the Worlds of Science Fiction, Fantasy and Horror* (Austin, Tex.: MonkeyBrain Books, 2004), 44. For VanderMeer's discussion of a related subject—the ersatz shadow arts movement known as the Romantic underground and the way in which it encompasses other movements such as romanticism, surrealism, the new weird, and interstitial fiction—see *Monstrous Creatures: Explorations of Fantasy through Essays, Articles and Reviews* (Bowie, Md.: Guide Dog Books, 2011), 31–36.

27. Miéville appears to privilege the former date, which seems appropriate given his central status in the new weird and the political bent of his fiction (which was directly inspired by the WTO protests of 1999). See Miéville, "Morbid Symptoms: An Interview with China Miéville," conducted by Benjamin Noys and Timothy S. Murphy, *Genre* 49, no. 2 (2016): 203. In a more recent interview, Miéville seems to disavow the relationship between the new weird and any actual historical event. See Miéville, "Not Just Some Viggo Mortensen of Desolated Left Politics: An Interview with China Miéville," conducted by Mark Bould, *Paradoxa* 28 (2016): 15–39. Benjamin Noys and Timothy S. Murphy appear to privilege the latter date given the reinvigoration Barker and Ligotti gave to weird fiction, which had largely been moribund since Lovecraft's death in 1937, a detrimental change in editor at *Weird Tales* in 1938, and the inability of new writers to work beyond homage to Lovecraft in this period. See Noys and Murphy, "Introduction: Old and New Weird," *Genre* 49, no. 2 (2016): 118–19.

28. S. T. Joshi, *The Weird Tale: Arthur Machen, Lord Dunsany, Algernon Blackwood, M. R. James, Ambrose Bierce, H. P. Lovecraft* (Austin: University of Texas Press, 1990).

29. H. P. Lovecraft, "Supernatural Horror in Literature," in *At the Mountains of Madness* (1936; reprint, New York: Modern Library, 2005), 103–73.

30. China Miéville, "Weird Fiction," in *The Routledge Companion to Science Fiction*, ed. Mark Bould et al. (London: Routledge, 2011), 511.

31. See China Miéville, "Reveling in Genre—An Interview with China Miéville," conducted by Joan Gordon, *Science Fiction Studies* 30, no. 3 (2003): 355–73.

32. See China Miéville, "Cognition as Ideology: A Dialectics of SF Theory," in *Red Planets: Marxism and Science Fiction*, ed. Mark Bould and China Miéville (Middletown, Conn.: Wesleyan University Press, 2009), 231–48.

33. The Castle books include *The Year of Our War* (2004), *No Present Like Time* (2005), *The Modern World* (2007; American title, *Dangerous Offspring*), *Above the Snowline* (2010), and *Fair Rebel* (2016).

34. See K. J. Bishop, *The Etched City* (2003), and Felix Gilman, *The Half-Made World* (2010) and *The Rise of Ransom City* (2012).

35. Lovecraft, "Supernatural Horror in Literature," 169.

36. China Miéville, "M. R. James and the Quantum Vampire: Weird; Hauntological: Versus And/or and And/or Or?," in *Collapse: Philosophical Research and Development—Volume 4*, ed. R. Mackay (Falmouth: Urbanomic, 2008), 105.

37. Miéville, "M. R. James and the Quantum Vampire," 112.

38. Mark McGurl, "The Posthuman Comedy," *Critical Inquiry*, no. 38 (2012): 533–53. McGurl claims that in fact it may be Lovecraft's pulpiness that makes him so relevant today.

39. Graham Harman, *Weird Realism: Lovecraft and Philosophy* (Winchester, U.K.: Zero Books, 2012), 5.

40. Carl H. Sederholm and Jeffrey Andrew Weinstock, "Introduction: Lovecraft Rising," in *The Age of Lovecraft*, eds. Sederholm and Weinstock (Minneapolis: University of Minnesota Press, 2016), 7–8.

41. Bruno Latour, *We Have Never Been Modern*, 5–8.

42. Noys and Murphy, "Introduction," 125.

43. Clive Barker, "In the Hills, the Cities," in *Books of Blood: Volumes One to Three* (New York: Berkley Books, 1998), 161–62.

44. VanderMeer, *Monstrous Creatures*, 9.

45. One can also trace the sympathetic monster, in part, to the neogothic of Anne Rice, whose *Interview with a Vampire* (1976) gave us a supernatural killer, Louis, forever wrestling with the morality of what he is and does. More recently, Glen Duncan has done similar work for a different monster in *The Last Werewolf* (2011). Our sympathy for these monsters, however, derives

from the way in which they succeed or fail to reconcile their monstrosity with their residual humanity and the norms it involves.

46. For Tolkien's account of secondary worlds and their relationship to belief, see J. R. R. Tolkien, *Tree and Leaf* (London: Allen & Unwin, 1964). The best single scholarly source on secondary worlds is Mark J. P. Wolf, *Building Imaginary Worlds: The Theory and History of Subcreation* (New York: Routledge, 2013). See also Mark J. P. Wolf, ed., *Revisiting Imaginary Worlds: A Subcreation Studies Anthology* (New York: Routledge, 2017); and Mark J. P. Wolf, ed., *The Routledge Companion to Imaginary Worlds* (New York: Routledge, 2018).

47. As this list suggests, it may be possible to roughly distinguish the two phases of the new weird—the one inaugurated by Barker in the 1980s and the one said to begin with *Perdido Street Station* in the 2000s—along the lines of primary/secondary world settings.

48. Timothy S. Murphy, "Supremely Monstrous Thought: H. P. Lovecraft and the Weirding of World Literature," *Genre* 49, no. 2 (July 2016): 162–63.

49. Mark McGurl, "The New Cultural Geology," *Twentieth-century Literature* 57, no. 3–4 (2011): 380.

50. Karl Marx, *The Portable Karl Marx*, ed. Eugene Kamenka (New York: Penguin, 1983), 287.

51. Karl Marx, *Capital: A Critique of Political Economy*, trans. Ben Fowkes (New York: Penguin, 1981), 102.

52. To be sure, there are moments in Marx that complicate this claim. Wark, for example, points out Marx's notion of "metabolic rift": "Labor pounds and wheedles rocks and soil, plants and animals, extracting molecular flows out of which shared life is made and remade. But those molecular flows do not return from whence they came." Wark, *Molecular Red*, xiii. In other words, labor does produce value out of nature, but nature retains a demonic capacity for misbehavior and acts according to its own "interests" in spite of human efforts to channel it. See Jason W. Moore, *Capitalism in the Web of Life: Ecology and the Accumulation of Capital* (New York: Verso, 2015), for further examination of this issue. In addition to metabolic rift, Marx's conception of species being suggests a more complex materiality than what we find in his accounts of history and historical materialism. See Nick Dyer-Witheford,

"1844/2004/2044: The Return of Species-Being," *Historical Materialism* 12, no. 4 (2004): 3–25.

53. In addition to the texts discussed here, for introductions to new materialism, see Stacy Alaimo and Susan J. Hekman, eds., *Material Feminisms* (Bloomington: Indiana University Press, 2008); Diana H. Coole and Samantha Frost, eds., *New Materialisms: Ontology, Agency, and Politics* (Durham, N.C.: Duke University Press, 2010); and Rick Dolphijn and Iris van der Tuin, *New Materialism: Interviews and Cartographies* (Ann Arbor, Mich.: Open Humanities Press, 2012).

54. Manuel De Landa, *A Thousand Years of Nonlinear History* (New York: Zone Books, 1997), 17.

55. De Landa, *Thousand Years*, 17.

56. John Durham Peters, *The Marvelous Clouds: Toward a Philosophy of Elemental Media* (Durham, N.C.: Duke University Press, 2015), 38.

57. Nicole Starosielski, *The Undersea Network* (Durham, N.C.: Duke University Press, 2015).

58. Jussi Parikka, *A Geology of Media* (Minneapolis: University of Minnesota Press, 2015).

59. Karen Barad, *Meeting the Universe Halfway: Quantum Physics and the Entanglement of Matter and Meaning* (Durham, N.C.: Duke University Press, 2007), 3. I do not mean to suggest here that these thinkers simply rely on an already stated given that they simply apply to new fields. Barad in particular—along with Elizabeth Grosz, Haraway, De Landa, and others— have been shaping the discourse now called new materialism since before there was a term to designate it.

60. Fredric Jameson, *The Political Unconscious: Narrative as a Socially Symbolic Act* (Ithaca, N.Y.: Cornell University Press, 1981), 20. Jameson cites from *The Communist Manifesto* in Marx, *Portable Karl Marx*, 203.

61. For example, Jameson claims that magic in fantasy is "a figure for the enlargement of human powers and their passage to the limit." The most "consequent fantasy," he argues, "is never some deployment of magic in the service of other narrative ends, but proposes a meditation on magic as such: on its capacities and its existential properties, on a kind of figural mapping of the active and productive subjectivity in its non-alienated state." Jameson, "Radical Fantasy," *Historical Materialism* 10, no. 4 (2002): 278–79. In other

words, magic can never just be magic, and the secondary world in which it exists must always stand in for an encoded primary world, even if in rendering the secondary world as such, the critic transforms it into a mythological state of Edenic bliss.

62. The problem of critique and the question of a postcritical moment have recently animated a great deal of discussion in the humanities and social sciences. See Marjorie Levinson, "Posthumous Critique," in *In Near Ruins: Cultural Theory at the End of the Century*, ed. Nicholas B. Dirks (Minneapolis: University of Minnesota Press, 1998), 257–94; Rita Felski, *The Limits of Critique* (Chicago: University of Chicago Press, 2015); Mitchum Huehls, *After Critique: Twenty-first-century Fiction in a Neoliberal Age* (New York: Oxford University Press, 2016); and Elizabeth S. Anker and Rita Felski, eds., *Critique and Postcritique* (Durham, N.C.: Duke University Press, 2017).

63. Ron Suskind, "Faith, Certainty and the Presidency of George W. Bush," *New York Times Magazine*, October 17, 2004, http://www.nytimes.com. It was later revealed that George W. Bush's advisor, Karl Rove, designated the reality-based community as such.

64. Bruno Latour, "Why Has Critique Run Out of Steam? From Matters of Fact to Matters of Concern," *Critical Inquiry* 30, no. 2 (2004): 245–46.

65. Yves Citton, "Fictional Attachments and Literary Weavings in the Anthropocene," *New Literary History* 47, no. 2–3 (2016): 310.

66. Bruno Latour, *An Inquiry into Modes of Existence: An Anthropology of the Moderns*, trans. Catherine Porter (Cambridge, Mass.: Harvard University Press, 2013), 238–39.

67. Citton, "Fictional Attachments," 314.

68. Gerry Canavan and Andrew Hageman, "Introduction: 'Global Weirding,'" *Paradoxa* 28 (2016): 7–13.

69. Darko Suvin, *Metamorphoses of Science Fiction: On the Poetics and History of a Literary Genre* (1979; reprint, New York: Peter Lang, 2016), 2.

70. Carl Freedman, *Critical Theory and Science Fiction* (Hanover: Wesleyan University Press, 2000). Despite criticism of his claims, Freedman doubles down on his arguments in *Art and Idea in the Novels of China Miéville* (Canterbury, U.K.: Gylphi, 2015).

71. Fredric Jameson, *Archaeologies of the Future: The Desire Called Utopia and Other Science Fictions* (New York: Verso, 2005), 292–95.

72. The *Blue Ant* trilogy comprises *Pattern Recognition* (2003), *Spook Country* (2007), and *Zero History* (2010).

2. LET ME TELL YOU ABOUT THE CITY

1. Veniss's development overlaps with that of Ambergris, which begins with *Dradin, in Love* in 1996. The Veniss texts were mainly published between 1991 and 2004.

2. Ghosh, *Great Derangement*, 58.

3. This discussion must unfortunately omit consideration of these texts' publication histories, except as briefly noted below. As mentioned in chapter 1, VanderMeer's career as a writer is characterized not only by extensive publication but also by publication in a wide variety of forms (novels, essays, writing guides, oddities, etc.); by publication in mainstream, small, and alternative presses and venues; and by consistent revision to previously published material. All of this complexity manifests in the Veniss texts, which take on several forms (novels, short stories, fragments); were published in a variety of venues (commercial presses, small presses, literary journals, popular magazines); and have undergone extensive revision even after publication. Such is especially the case with the 2004 collection *Secret Life*, where many of the Veniss short stories are collected, which was reissued as *Secret Life: The Select Fire Remix* (Canton, Ohio: Prime Books, 2006). This newer paperback edition is quite different from the hardcover in terms of the selection of texts (several of which are not included in the hardcover, including one of the Veniss stories), but also in terms of its organization (for example, the title story is split up into sections that appear between the other stories in the newer edition, and the entire volume is framed by a narrative that fictionalizes its own development). For a publication history of most of the Veniss texts and their various editions, see "Series: Veniss," Internet Science Fiction Database, http://www.isfdb.org. The publication histories of the Veniss texts not listed here can be found in "Summary Bibliography: Jeff VanderMeer," Internet Speculative Fiction Database, http://www.isfdb.org.

4. "The Sea, Mendeho, and Moonlight," in *Secret Life* (Urbana, Ill.: Gryphon Press, 2004), 56–62; "Veniss Exposed: Precursors and Epiphanies (An Afterword)," in *Veniss Underground* (London: Tor, 2003), 165–77. This story, along with a note about its relationship to the Veniss milieu, originally

appeared in the U.K. edition of *Veniss Underground* and has appeared in at least two new editions of the novel since its original publication. It was not included in the original U.S. edition of the novel I am working from here. "Flesh," *Fear*, May 1991, 37–40. "Flesh" is perhaps the most difficult text to situate in the overall Veniss milieu insofar as it is the one text not set in Veniss or in the surrounding area. Rather, it is set on one of the colonial starships that take off from and land in the canals surrounding Veniss, as mentioned in "The Sea, Mendeho, and Moonlight," and only occasionally refers to the milieu and the events that take place there. The VanderMeer bibliography at the Internet Science Fiction Database does not list it among the Veniss texts, and it seems to have at most an oblique relationship to the rest of the texts I list here. In fact, it seems to contradict some facts of the milieu as established in the other texts (about the origins of the meerkats, for example), even beyond the apparent inconsistencies or discontinuities at the center of the present argument. *Veniss Underground* (Canton, Ohio: Prime Books, 2003); "Detectives and Cadavers," in *Secret Life*, 147–57; "Jessible and the Metal Dragon," in *Secret Life: The Select Fire Remix* (Canton, Ohio: Prime Books, 2006), 290–95. As cited here, this fragment is part of a note to "A Heart for Lucretia," a note that is only included in the paperback edition of *Secret Life*. "A Heart for Lucretia," in *Secret Life*, 229–39; "Balzac's War," in *Secret Life*, 196–228; "The City," in *Secret Life*, 285–93. "Three Days in a Border Town," in *The Third Bear* (San Francisco, Calif.: Tachyon Publications, 2010), 177–98. As with "Flesh," the bibliography of Veniss texts cited in note 3 does not include "Three Days in a Border Town" despite clear references to entities that clearly belong to the milieu. Only in "Three Days" is "The City" revealed to be definitively part of the milieu. I am grateful to Jeff VanderMeer for drawing my attention to this final Veniss text.

5. VanderMeer, "Detectives and Cadavers," 148.

6. VanderMeer, "Sea, Mendeho, and Moonlight," 61.

7. VanderMeer, "Veniss Exposed," 166.

8. VanderMeer, "Detectives and Cadavers," 150.

9. In "Veniss Exposed," VanderMeer hints at the idea that the story of the Veniss milieu is Quin's story insofar as his influence is felt in all of the texts that follow (even "Flesh," which again only makes passing reference to the milieu). Although such a claim may seem rather humanist, the fact of Quin's

disappearance and the fact that his creations so transform the world—far more so than any creation of the mad scientists of the nineteenth-century gothic, for example—suggests again the manner in which the milieu resists such notions.

10. At the conclusion of "Veniss Exposed," a story which seems to have been written early in the development of the milieu but published only much later, VanderMeer offers the following on these difficulties: "And that is the story of Quin, gleaned from a few fragments of short story I never finished (and which may or may not match the reality of [*Veniss Underground*]). In a sense, what makes it to the printed page is always a fragment of something larger, whether because you wrote character studies in aid of character development, or because inspiration left you at a critical time, or because a scene didn't really belong in the novel after all—even though somewhere out there, in a universe where everything literary is real, that scene actually occurred, because life (unlike fiction) isn't all about dramatic potential" (174). This explanation satisfies in terms of the writer's craft and the realities of writing for publication. It does not, however, suffice for critics who can only deal with what they have in front of them. The Veniss texts can be productively read if we understand them in terms of their resistance to setting rather than taking this resistance as merely accidental or merely as the result of the impossibility of completely coherent world building. To demand perfection in such endeavors is to measure the success of a fictional world in terms of its reduction to or deduction from the primary world.

11. On the subject of consistency in world building, see Wolf, *Building Imaginary Worlds*, 43–48; and Rodrigo Lessa and João Araújo, "World Consistency," in Wolfe, *Routledge Companion to Imaginary Worlds*. See also the discussions of "retroactive continuity" in Wolf, *Building Imaginary Worlds*, 212–16; and William Proctor, "Retroactive Continuity and Reboots," in Wolf, *Routledge Companion to Imaginary Worlds*.

12. VanderMeer, *Veniss Underground*, 10.

13. VanderMeer, *Veniss Underground*, 11.

14. VanderMeer, *Veniss Underground*, 100.

15. To put this line of argument in conversation with a still relevant analysis of contemporary literature, we might say that the Veniss texts neither ask the epistemological questions of modernist fiction nor the ontological questions of postmodernist fiction, as described in Brian McHale, *Postmodernist Fiction*

(New York: Routledge, 1987). For McHale, questions such as "what world is this?" suggest a shift in the poetics of fiction, one that moves away from questions such as "how do I know this world?" The Veniss texts, read alongside McGurl's cultural geology, suggest that even questions of ontology assume a setting in which such questions and the terms they comprise (such as "world") can take on meaning for human being.

16. My description of the three main genres of fantastika here draws heavily on and adapts John Clute's discussion of their respective structures in various places. For an overall introduction to these structures, see John Clute, *Pardon This Intrusion: Fantastika in the World Storm* (Essex: Beccon Publications, 2011), 19–31. For more detailed descriptions of the parts thereof, see: the entries on "Wrongness," "Thinning," "Recognition," "Healing," and "Story," in John Clute and John Grant, *The Encyclopedia of Fantasy* (New York: St. Martin's Griffin, 1999); the entry on "Conceptual Breakthrough" in John Clute and Peter Nicholls, eds., *The Encyclopedia of Science Fiction* (New York: St. Martin's Griffin, 1995); and the entries on "Sighting," "Thickening," "Revel," "Aftermath," "Horror," "Bound Fantastic," and "Free Fantastic" in John Clute, *The Darkening Garden: A Short Lexicon of Horror* (Cauheegan, Wisc.: Payseur & Schmidt, 2006). Clute himself is drawing on numerous writers and thinkers, the most significant of which in the present discussion is Darko Suvin, whose conceptualizations of the novum and of cognitive estrangement closely associate science fiction with historicist and critical thought and whose denigration of supernatural genres (especially fantasy, but by extension horror) relates the other subgenres of fantastika to such thought negatively. See Suvin, *Metamorphoses of Science Fiction*. I develop the relationship I identify between science fiction and fantasy here in "'A place I have never seen': Possibility, Genre, Politics, and China Miéville's *The Scar*," *Journal of the Fantastic in the Arts* 27, no. 1 (2016): 68–88; and more extensively in *Here at the End of All Things: Fantasy after History* (Baltimore, Md.: Johns Hopkins University Press, forthcoming).

17. Peter Sloterdjik, *Bubbles: Spheres Volume I: Microspherology*, trans. Wieland Hoban (Los Angeles: Semiotext(e), 2011), 9–10.

18. Steven Shaviro offers readings of science fiction texts whose tendencies are antithetical to those I identify here. See Shaviro, *Discognition* (London: Repeater Books, 2016).

19. I owe this point to Peter Sloterdjik's discussion of the age of exploration in which he identifies the ship as "the mobilized nest or the absolute house" and the task of exploration as "a mobilization of the interior." See Sloterdjik, *In the World Interior of Capital: For a Philosophical Theory of Globalization*, trans. Wieland Hoban (Cambridge: Polity Press, 2013), 122.

20. These are of course matters addressed by Quentin Meillassoux and other speculative realists. For Meillassoux, there can be statements that are true without any subjectivity, outside of what he calls the correlationist circle. Such statements include ones such as, "The earth formed 4.5 billion years ago." However, it nonetheless seems that, whatever truth they possess or denote, these statements cannot be meaningful, if what is meaningful must be so in a limited, anthropomorphic, and anthropocentric context. For his discussion of the true statements of math and science, see Meillassoux, *After Finitude: An Essay on the Necessity of Contingency* (New York: Continuum, 2009), especially chap. 1. Although I find Meillassoux's overall argument compelling, I also find that, like horror, he leaves the human too exposed in what he calls "the great outdoors," where there seems to be little room for politics or other human concerns. My goal here is not to argue yet again that humanity deludes itself and thus disappoint humanity from its self-interested position in the world. Rather, like Latour and (I think) VanderMeer, I wish to connect humanity and its interests to what lie outside those interests. Doing so will transform these interests, but this transformation requires concern rather than facts (or truth).

21. McGurl, "New Cultural Geology," 3–4.

22. Ghosh, *Great Derangement*, 61.

23. Ghosh, *Great Derangement*, 61.

24. Ghosh, *Great Derangement*, 62.

25. Ghosh, *Great Derangement*, 59, emphasis added.

26. Edward W. Said, *Culture and Imperialism* (New York: Vintage Books, 1994), 89.

27. Frank Kermode offers perhaps the most famous argument about how endpoints produce meaning for human narratives in *The Sense of an Ending: Studies in the Theory of Fiction* (Oxford: Oxford University Press, 1967).

28. Said, *Culture and Imperialism*, 87.

29. Ghosh, *Great Derangement*, 62.

30. Rob Nixon, *Slow Violence and the Environmentalism of the Poor* (Cambridge, Mass.: Harvard University Press, 2013).

31. Murphy, "Supremely Monstrous Thought." See also Latour's use of the term "geostory" in "Agency at the Time of the Anthropocene."

32. Gayatri Chakravorty Spivak, *A Critique of Postcolonial Reason: Toward a History of the Vanishing Present* (Cambridge, Mass.: Harvard University Press, 1999), 269–311.

33. VanderMeer, "Balzac's War," 197.

34. VanderMeer, "Balzac's War," 198.

35. VanderMeer, "Balzac's War," 225.

36. VanderMeer, "Balzac's War," 206.

37. VanderMeer, "Heart for Lucretia," 239. VanderMeer first makes this point about the relationship between myth and science fiction, using identical language, in an essay on Cordwainer Smith originally published in 2002, several years before *Secret Life*. See VanderMeer, *Why Should I Cut Your Throat?*, 245.

38. VanderMeer, "Three Days in a Border Town," 181.

39. VanderMeer, "Three Days in a Border Town," 185.

40. VanderMeer, "City," 293.

41. Although there are some gendered pronouns in the story, the detective's gender remains unclear and gender itself seems irrelevant to the daily lives of the story's characters. I use feminine pronouns here simply as a default.

42. VanderMeer, "City," 287.

43. VanderMeer, "City," 288. Despite its insistence that the city belongs to the Veniss milieu, "Three Days in a Border Town" likewise represents the city in resolutely obscure terms: "There is but one City in all the world. Ever it travels across the face of the Earth, both as promise and as curse. None of us shall but glimpse it from the corner of one eye" (178). To this obscurity the story adds the border towns, where the humans who long for the city live in imitation of it: "Every border town is the same; in observing unspoken fealty to the City, it dare not replicate the City too closely. By necessity, every border town replicates its brothers and sisters. In speech. In habits" (183). The homogeneity of the border towns with respect to one another, and their asymptotic relationship to the city, again suggest a resistance to setting. No two border towns can be distinguished from one another. They may only be

partly distinguished from the city, which remains always unavailable as a definite referent through which such a distinction might be made.

44. VanderMeer, "City," 289.

45. VanderMeer, "City," 292.

46. VanderMeer, "Detectives and Cadavers," 155.

47. VanderMeer, "City," 289.

3. NO ONE MAKES IT OUT, THERE MAY BE A WAY

1. Jeff VanderMeer, *Shriek: An Afterword* (New York: Tor, 2007), 17.

2. Jeff VanderMeer, *City of Saints and Madmen* (New York: Bantam Books, 2006). Where I cite from *City of Saints and Madmen*'s Appendix, the pagination of which does not continue from the novel's first four sections, I attempt to make clear which of the Appendix's texts the cited text can be found in. Where possible, I also note the page from that text.

3. VanderMeer, *Shriek*, 305.

4. VanderMeer, *Shriek*, 16, 32, 43, 74.

5. VanderMeer, *Shriek*, 94.

6. VanderMeer, *Shriek*, 95.

7. VanderMeer, *Shriek*, 96.

8. VanderMeer, *Shriek*, 96–97.

9. VanderMeer, *Shriek*, 339.

10. VanderMeer, *Shriek*, 335.

11. VanderMeer, *Shriek*, 336.

12. VanderMeer, *Shriek*, 318, 250–51.

13. VanderMeer, *Shriek*, 325.

14. Because the world in which Ambergris exists is never named, I shall refer to both the city and the world as Ambergris, making clear which I am referring to if the distinction is not clear in specific instances of this usage.

15. Although the publication history of the Ambergris texts serves to underscore several of the points I will make in this chapter, the complexity of this publication history precludes an extensive account of it here, although I will briefly allude to it as necessary in what follows. The Ambergris narrative comprises three novels—*City of Saints and Madmen, Shriek: An Afterword*, and *Finch*—and numerous shorter texts of various form. *City of Saints and Madmen* exists in three editions: a first edition published by Cosmos

Books/Wildside Press in 2001 that includes only the four novellas that each subsequent edition includes at their beginnings; a second, hardcover, print-on-demand edition published by Prime Books in 2002 that includes most of the Ambergris materials that existed at that time; and what seems to be a definitive edition published by Tor in 2004, which includes a few more texts than the Prime edition but excludes certain aspects of that edition (the vignette found only on the dust jacket, the full encryption of "The Man Who Had No Eyes"). For VanderMeer's discussion of the difficulties of producing the Prime Books edition of the novel, which includes a great deal of information about the differences amongst the various editions, see "City of Saints and Madmen: The Untold Story," in Why Should I Cut Your Throat?, 51–83. The publication histories of Shriek and Finch are significantly less complex. The differences between the standard and special editions of the former involve the inclusion with the special edition of a soundtrack by the Church (whom VanderMeer singles out in Shriek's music acknowledgments, which describe the albums and bands he listened to while composing various scenes). See the archived website for Shriek: Jeff VanderMeer, Shriek: An Afterword—The Official Website, https://web. archive.org/web/20170516233300/http://www.shriekthenovel.com/. Finch's three editions, one standard and two special, also diverge in terms of what they include as bonus materials. Although some of these extras, such as a chapbook of Fragments of a Drowned City (Finch's original title, when it told a rather different story), are interesting, they do not much affect the narrative itself. See Jeff VanderMeer, "Rebel Samizdat and Heretic Editions: Excerpt and Limited Details for Jeff VanderMeer's Novel Finch," Borne Central, August 29, 2009, http://www.jeffvandermeer.com. Beyond these novels, most of the fragments that make up City of Saints and Madmen were published before their appearance there, sometimes in the form of limited edition chapbooks or as found objects supposedly from the world of Ambergris. Several early versions of these texts, along with a fragment that eventually appeared in Shriek, were collected in the hardcover edition of Secret Life. This edition of Secret Lives also includes two bits of Ambergris ephemera: the short story "Corpse Mouth and Spore Nose," taken from Fragments of a Drowned City, and "The Festival of the Freshwater Squid," which imagines one of Ambergris's signature events as a local holiday in

Florida and rewrites numerous Ambergris characters as the denizens of that state. For a comprehensive list of the Ambergris texts and their publication histories, see "Series: Ambergris," Internet Science Fiction Database, http://www.isfdb.org/.

16. Mark Z. Danielewski, *House of Leaves* (New York: Pantheon, 2000).

17. Clute and Grant, *Encyclopedia of Fantasy*, 738, emphasis modified.

18. On the subject of completeness in world building, see Wolf, *Building Imaginary Worlds*, 38–43; and Benjamin J. Robertson, "World Completeness," in Wolf, *Routledge Companion to Imaginary Worlds*. On the subject of consistency, see Wolf, *Building Imaginary Worlds*, 43–48; and Lessa and Araújo, "World Consistency."

19. At the same time, fantasy scholars such as Farah Mendlesohn have suggested that fantasy or the fantastic is actually the literary norm and that realism or mimeticism are the aberrations insofar as they implicitly claim to reflect a world rather than build one. Mendlesohn writes, with regard to what she calls the immersive fantasy, "that all literature builds worlds, but some genres are more honest about it than others. Mimetic literature, that fabulous conjuration of 'the real,' is the product of a cumulative bible." Mendlesohn, *Rhetorics of Fantasy* (Middletown, Conn.: Wesleyan University Press, 2008), 59.

20. J. R. R. Tolkien, *The Two Towers* (New York: Ballantine Books, 1965), 408.

21. Clute and Grant, *Encyclopedia of Fantasy*, 804. Compare this discussion with the entry on conceptual breakthrough in Clute and Nicholls, *Encyclopedia of Science Fiction*, 254–57; and Clute's comparison of the grammars of fantasy, science fiction, and horror in *Pardon This Intrusion*, 19–31.

22. Tolkien, *Tree and Leaf*, 36.

23. China Miéville asserts that sophistry is also at work in science fiction, contrary to claims by its historical materialist apologists. See Miéville, "Cognition as Ideology," 231–48.

24. Mendlesohn's account of the rhetoric of the portal-quest fantasy, which renders impossible all critical thought with regard to such narration, is the best discussion of the problem of representation in fantasy; see *Rhetorics of Fantasy*, 1–58. See also the discussion of Story, which makes clear the degree to which fantasy aspires to a total coherence only possible in a construction that denies its own constructedness, in Clute and Grant, *Encyclopedia of Fantasy*, 899–901.

25. I have no wish to weigh in on past or present arguments about the true meaning or absolute necessity of such terms as postmodern, postmodernity, postmodernist, or postmodernism. Suffice it to say that I generally find Fredric Jameson's account of postmodernism as the "cultural logic of late capitalism" the most coherent and useful definition and articulation of the concepts I loosely group here. That said, I use the term "postmodernist" here as a naive proxy for the Anglo-American experimental fictions of the past half century produced by such writers as Thomas Pynchon, John Barth, Kathy Acker, Toni Morrison, Ishmael Reed, and Don DeLillo. Any reader interested in the debate about whether this term reflects some actual constellation of texts, or the argument over the possibility of describing a true postmodernist poetics or aesthetics, already knows where to find it. For an excellent account of the afterlives of this debate, see the essays collected in Jason Gladstone, Andrew Hoberek, and Daniel Worden, eds., *Postmodern/ Postwar and After: Rethinking American Literature* (Iowa City: University of Iowa Press, 2016).

26. McHale, *Postmodernist Fiction*, 9.

27. McHale, *Postmodernist Fiction*, 10.

28. Fredric Jameson, "Postmodernism and Consumer Society," in *The Anti-aesthetic: Essays on Postmodern Culture*, ed. Hal Foster (New York: New Press, 1998), 114.

29. Ryan Vu contradicts my argument here when he demonstrates the manner in which, in a postgeneric era such as ours, the fantasy text becomes a game and thus a template for certain recent cultural products, such as the prestige television of HBO's *Game of Thrones*. See Vu, "Fantasy after Representation: D&D, Game of Thrones, and Postmodern World-Building," *Extrapolation* 58, no. 2–3 (2017): 273–301.

30. VanderMeer, *Monstrous Creatures*, 238.

31. Mitchum Huehls, "The Post-theory Theory Novel," *Contemporary Literature* 56, no. 2 (2015): 282.

32. Huehls, "Post-theory Theory Novel," 287.

33. Huehls, "Post-theory Theory Novel," 288.

34. Two of the best examples of such scholarship are Kate Marshall, "What Are the Novels of the Anthropocene? American Fiction in Geological Time," *American Literary History* 27, no. 3 (2015): 523–38; and Tobias Boes and

Kate Marshall, "Writing the Anthropocene: An Introduction" *Minnesota Review* 2014, no. 83 (2014): 60–72.

35. Mitchum Huehls, "Risking Complicity," Arcade: Literature, the Humanities, and the World, November 9, 2015, http://arcade.stanford.edu.

36. J. R. R. Tolkien, *The Fellowship of the Ring* (New York: Ballantine Books, 1965), 12–13.

37. E. R. Eddison, *The Worm Ouroboros* (1922; reprint, Mineola, N.Y.: Dover, 2006), ix.

38. Stephen R. Donaldson, *Epic Fantasy in the Modern World* (Kent, Ohio: Kent State University Press, 1986).

39. Carl Freedman, "A Note on Marxism and Fantasy," *Historical Materialism* 10, no. 4 (2002): 263.

40. When sections of *City of Saints and Madmen* have been published as stand-alone texts, I will italicize their titles. In the cases of *The Hoegbotton Guide to the Early History of Ambergris*, and *Dradin, in Love*, this italicization makes additional sense because of the texts' publication history in Ambergris.

41. VanderMeer, *Saints, King Squid*, 34.

42. In its tone, Shriek's commentary in *The Hoegbotton Guide to the Early History of Ambergris* and *Shriek: An Afterword* is strikingly similar to that of VanderMeer's reviews and discussions of the state of genre fiction. Compare Shriek's criticisms of other historians and writers in these two texts to VanderMeer's: "The knock on Steve Aylett, when there's been one, is that he's too clever for his own good. After reading Aylett's new story collection, *Toxicology*, I wish more writers were too clever for their own good—it sure beats being lumped in with all those other writers who are too stupid for their own good" and "Every time a critic writes a good review to curry favor or a publication cuts a negative review because of some constituency to be mollified, the field loses a little more of its vitality" (VanderMeer, *Why Should I Cut Your Throat?*, 188, 224). See also the entirety of VanderMeer's assault on horror publishing (226–43).

43. VanderMeer, *Saints*, 330.

44. VanderMeer discusses the difficulty of encoding "The Man with No Eyes" in *Why Should I Cut Your Throat?*, 67–70.

45. See, for example, the note to "Learning to Leave the Flesh" in Jeff Vander-Meer, *Secret Life* (Urbana, Ill.: Gryphon Press, 2004), 125–26, which reveals

the non-Ambergrisian origin and thematics of that story as well as some information about how it finally came to be included in *City of Saints and Madmen.*

46. See VanderMeer, *Why Should I Cut Your Throat?*, 100. See also VanderMeer's discussion of *House of Leaves* in *Monstrous Creatures*, 176–78.

47. VanderMeer has told me that he had read *House of Leaves* by the time he designed the hardcover edition of the novel (e-mail, September 20, 2017).

48. VanderMeer, *Why Should I Cut Your Throat?*, 96.

49. N. Katherine Hayles, *Writing Machines* (Cambridge, Mass.: MIT Press, 2002), 110.

50. See Mark B. N. Hansen, *Bodies in Code: Interfaces with Digital Media* (New York: Routledge, 2006), 221–24.

51. Bram Stoker, *Dracula*, ed. Roger Luckhurst (1897; reprint, Oxford: Oxford University Press, 2011), 351. On *Dracula* as a consideration of media, see Friedrich A. Kittler, "Dracula's Legacy," in *Literature, Media, Information Systems: Essays*, ed. John Johnston (New York: Routledge, 2013), 50–84.

52. Like *Dradin, in Love*, the *Guide* also appeared before its inclusion in *City of Saints and Madmen* as a chapbook published in 1999.

53. VanderMeer, *Shriek*, 303.

54. VanderMeer, *Saints*, 150.

55. VanderMeer, *Shriek*, 70.

56. VanderMeer, *Saints*, 171, my emphases.

57. VanderMeer, *Shriek*, 34.

58. VanderMeer, *Shriek*, 33.

59. VanderMeer, *Shriek*, 260.

60. This photograph appears on the cover of several editions of the novel and on page 341 of the edition from which I am working.

61. VanderMeer, *Shriek*, 340.

62. VanderMeer, *Shriek*, 67.

63. VanderMeer, *Shriek*, 63.

64. VanderMeer, *Shriek*, 281.

65. VanderMeer, *Finch*, 306.

66. VanderMeer, *Finch*, 306.

67. Reprinted in VanderMeer, *Monstrous Creatures*, 231.

4. THERE IS NOTHING BUT BORDER. THERE IS NO BORDER.

1. The Southern Reach trilogy comprises *Annihilation, Authority,* and *Acceptance* (New York: Farrar, Straus and Giroux, 2014). The publication history of the trilogy is considerably less complicated than that of either the Veniss or the Ambergris materials. In addition to the three volumes from which I work here, the trilogy was also published in a single-volume edition: *Area X: The Southern Reach Trilogy* (New York: Farrar, Straus and Giroux, 2014). There appear to have been some special items, such as a map, available at certain events, and several of VanderMeer's short stories of the decade leading up to the trilogy anticipate the trilogy's themes or even seem to be studies for certain aspects of the trilogy, but mainly the story of Area X is contained in these three volumes.

2. VanderMeer, *Annihilation,* 94.

3. VanderMeer, *Authority,* 35.

4. VanderMeer, *Acceptance,* 41.

5. VanderMeer, *Authority,* 290.

6. VanderMeer, *Annihilation,* 25.

7. VanderMeer, *Annihilation,* 8.

8. VanderMeer, *Annihilation,* 10.

9. VanderMeer, *Acceptance,* 5.

10. Roger Luckhurst, "Afterweird: Konvolut N+1: City/Slither," in *China Miéville: Critical Essays,* ed. Caroline Edwards and Tony Venezia (Canterbury, U.K.: Gylphi, 2015), 280.

11. VanderMeer, *Authority,* 135.

12. VanderMeer, *Annihilation,* 98; *Acceptance,* 32.

13. VanderMeer, *Authority,* 294–95.

14. Elizabeth A. Povinelli, *Geontologies: A Requiem to Late Liberalism* (Durham, N.C.: Duke University Press, 2016).

15. VanderMeer, *Acceptance,* 283.

16. VanderMeer, *Authority,* 305–6.

17. I do not mean to suggest that human constructions possess no force. Anyone who exists as, for example, a person marginalized by way of race, gender, or sexuality will be well aware of the force such constructions possess. My point here is that these constructions matter little or not at all to the material forces

embodied by Area X or the Anthropocene (even if the two cannot be reduced to one another).

18. Eugene Thacker, *Tentacles Longer Than Night* (Winchester, U.K.: Zero Books, 2015), 114–15.

19. Shaviro, *Discognition*, 10–11.

20. VanderMeer, *Annihilation*, 159.

21. VanderMeer, *Authority*, 262.

22. VanderMeer, *Acceptance*, 225.

23. VanderMeer, *Acceptance*, 225.

24. On the friend/enemy distinction as the basis of politics, see Carl Schmitt, *The Concept of the Political*, trans. George Schwab (Chicago: University of Chicago Press, 1996). For development and complication of this sort of boundary drawing, see Giorgio Agamben, *Homo Sacer: Sovereign Power and Bare Life*, trans. Daniel Heller-Roazen (Stanford, Calif.: Stanford University Press, 1998); and Agamben, *The Open: Man and Animal*, trans. Kevin Attell (Stanford, Calif: Stanford University Press, 2004).

25. Eugene Thacker, *In the Dust of This Planet* (Winchester, U.K.: Zero Books, 2011), 7.

26. Luckhurst, "Afterweird," 279.

27. VanderMeer, *Annihilation*, 130.

28. VanderMeer, *Acceptance*, 186.

29. Here, as elsewhere in this book, my understanding of *geos* and its meaning in the formulation "geopolitical" is informed by the notion of geoliterature— that is, a world literature not determined by abstract lines on the surface of the globe—in Murphy, "Supremely Monstrous Thought."

30. The literature on biopower and biopolitics, like that on the Anthropocene, constitutes a freestanding discourse in its own right and thus cannot be summarized here. One of the most popular shorthands for biopower, that it involves the power "a power to *foster* life or *disallow* it to the point of death," was formulated by Michel Foucault in *The History of Sexuality*, trans. Robert Hurley (New York: Vintage Books, 1990), 138. This issue is further explored in Agamben's *Homo Sacer* and many other texts.

31. Jeffrey T. Nealon, *Plant Theory: Biopower and Vegetable Life* (Stanford, Calif.: Stanford University Press, 2016).

32. Alexander G. Weheliye, *Habeas Viscus: Racializing Assemblages, Biopolitics, and Black Feminist Theories of the Human* (Durham, N.C.: Duke University Press, 2014).

33. Eugene Thacker, *After Life* (Chicago: University of Chicago Press, 2010).

34. Povinelli, *Geontologies*, 4.

35. Povinelli, *Geontologies*, 5.

36. These are only two of numerous definitions of "area" offered by the *Oxford English Dictionary* (http://www.oed.com/), most of which suggest that areas must have human uses or other relationships to human knowledge and being.

37. VanderMeer, *Annihilation*, 129.

38. VanderMeer, *Annihilation*, 157.

39. VanderMeer, *Annihilation*, 19.

40. VanderMeer, *Acceptance*, 54.

41. The term "cosmic indifference" comes up often in informal discussions of Lovecraft and the weird, although outside of journals and other venues that specialize in Lovecraft studies this precise formulation does not often appear in print. Sederhom and Weinstock use the term, but do not dwell on it, in their introduction to *Age of Lovecraft*, 14. Scott Selisker attributes it, or at least the concept it expresses, to Mark McGurl in "'Stutter-Stop Flash-Bulb Strange': GMOs and the Aesthetics of Scale in Paolo Bacigalupi's *The Windup Girl*," *Science Fiction Studies* 42, no. 3 (2015): 501. McGurl certainly expresses something along these lines with regard to Lovecraft and related writers and movements, but does not use the precise term, in "The Posthuman Comedy," *Critical Inquiry*, no. 38 (2012): 533–53, or "The New Cultural Geology," *Twentieth-century Literature* 57, no. 3–4 (2011): 380–90.

42. My use of the prefix "a-" is inspired by Timothy Murphy's description of "amodernism," which is neither modernism nor postmodernism despite having developed in the same cultural and historical milieu as those movements. See Timothy S. Murphy, *Wising Up the Marks: The Amodern William Burroughs* (Berkeley: University of California Press, 1997), 16–45. China Miéville makes frequent use of the "ab-" in his fiction and thought, as in, for example, "abdead" and "abcanny." For further discussion of the "ab-," see Sherryl Vint, "Ab-Realism: Fractal Language and Social Change," in Edwards and Venezia, *China Miéville*, 39–59; and Mark P. Williams, "Abnatural Resources: Collective Experience, Community and Commonality

from Embassytown to New Crobuzon," in Edwards and Venezia, *China Miéville*, 239–64. See also the brief discussion of Charles Peirce's notion of abduction in relation to speculation in Shaviro, *Discognition*, 12–13.

43. Although this flatness is related to the flatness espoused in Gilles Deleuze and Félix Guattari's discussion of the rhizome in *A Thousand Plateaus: Capitalism and Schizophrenia*, trans. Brian Massumi (Minneapolis: University of Minnesota Press, 1987), and that elaborated by Levi Bryant in *The Democracy of Objects* (Ann Arbor, Mich.: Open Humanities Press, 2011), it differs in important respects. Although this flatness is one that "fills[s] or occup[ies] all of [its] dimensions" (Deleuze and Guattari, *Thousand Plateaus*, 9), it does not connect, actually or virtually, with everything else as do rhizomatic structures. Although it decenters the human, as in Bryant's flat ontology, it does not place every object on precisely the same footing. Area X does not have a privileged position with regard to the human or anything else, but it does not have a comparable one either.

44. Povinelli, *Geontologies*, 45.

45. Leo Braudy, *Haunted: On Ghosts, Witches, Vampires, Zombies, and Other Monsters of the Natural and Supernatural Worlds* (New Haven, Conn.: Yale University Press, 2016), 26.

46. Jorge Luis Borges, "The Analytical Language of John Wilkins" (1942), in *Other Inquisitions (1937–1952)*, trans. Ruth L. C. Simms (Austin: University of Texas Press, 1964).

47. Braudy, *Haunted*, 234, 244.

48. Lovecraft's racism remains vexing for critics. Harman ignores it in *Weird Realism*. China Miéville offers a fairly nuanced, if brief, account of it in his introduction to Lovecraft, *At the Mountains of Madness*, xi–xxv. Longtime Lovecraft scholar and editor S. T. Joshi has recently defended it—against so-called social justice warriors who campaigned the World Fantasy Awards to no longer use Lovecraft's bust for its trophies—as being a product of its times. Fortunately, he lost that battle. See Alison Flood, "H. P. Lovecraft Biographer Rages against Ditching of Author as Fantasy Prize Emblem," *Guardian*, November 11, 2015, https://www.theguardian.com.

49. See Miéville, "M. R. James and the Quantum Vampire."

50. Lovecraft, "Supernatural Horror in Literature," 169.

51. Harman, *Weird Realism*.

52. H. P. Lovecraft, *The Call of Cthulhu and Other Weird Stories*, ed. S. T. Joshi (New York: Penguin Books, 1999), 141.

53. Lovecraft, *At the Mountains of Madness*, 91.

54. I should note that, of course, Lovecraft does not represent the sum total of the weird and that other writers, such as William Hope Hodgson, went about describing their monsters in quite different ways. Consider, for example, the following description from Hodgson's *The Night Land* (London: Ballantine, 1972): "Beyond these, South and West of them, was the enormous bulk of the South-West Watcher, and from the ground rose what we named the Eye Beam—a single ray of grey light, which came up out of the ground, and lit the right eye of the monster" (35). Rather than an excess of description, Hodgson deploys a self-reflexive one. What lies "South and West" is "the South-West Watcher" and what lights "the right eye of the monster" is called the "Eye Beam." Whereas Lovecraft describes the indescribable through contradiction or geometric impossibility, Hodgson's language suggests that things and their descriptions are utterly the same, beyond a form of signification that maintains that this thing in appearance is like some other thing.

55. Benjamin Noys, "Horror Temporis," *Collapse IV* (Falmouth, U.K.: Urbanomic, 2008), 278.

56. Noys, "Horror Temporis," 279.

57. In an excellent example of the contemporary weird, Victor LaValle rewrites "The Horror at Red Hook" and subverts its overt racism. See LaValle, *The Ballad of Black Tom* (New York: Tor, 2016).

58. VanderMeer, *Annihilation*, 159.

59. See, e.g., Noys and Murphy, "Introduction"; Luckhurst, "Afterweird"; and Carroll, "The Terror and the Terroir." Carl Freedman goes so far as to say that China Miéville's fiction is not only political in orientation but also explicitly didactic in *Art and Idea in the Novels of China Miéville*.

60. VanderMeer, *Annihilation*, 155.

61. VanderMeer, *Authority*, 315.

62. VanderMeer, *Acceptance*, 337.

63. VanderMeer has long resided in Florida, and Florida has figured in his fiction before. He discusses his relationship with the state in several places, notably in "The Peculiar States of Florida: Laura van den Berg and Jeff VanderMeer

in Conversation," interview conducted by Laura van den Berg, FSG: Work in Progress, https://fsgworkinprogress.com.

64. VanderMeer, *Annihilation*, 94.

65. VanderMeer, *Acceptance*, 65.

66. VanderMeer, *Authority*, 240.

67. VanderMeer, *Authority*, 37.

68. Carroll, "The Terror and the Terroir," 78. "Capitalocene" is Jason W. Moore's term for the Anthropocene, coined to highlight the fact that humanity strictly speaking is less responsible for catastrophic climate change than capitalism and its institutions. Moore, "Anthropocene or Capitalocene: Nature, History, and the Crisis of Capitalism," in *Anthropocene or Capitalocene? Nature, History, and the Crisis of Capitalism*, ed. Jason W. Moore (Oakland, Calif.: PM Press, 2016), 1–13. See also Moore, *Capitalism in the Web of Life*.

69. VanderMeer, *Annihilation*, 186–87.

70. VanderMeer, *Acceptance*, 24–25.

71. VanderMeer, *Acceptance*, 59.

72. VanderMeer, *Authority*, 297.

73. Chakrabarty has famously called for a consciousness of humanity's status as a species but importantly understands this "species being" as part and parcel of a geological force rather than as a properly political stance. Chakrabarty, "Postcolonial Studies."

74. Tom Cohen, Claire Colebrook, and J. Hillis Miller, *Twilight of the Anthropocene Idols* (Ann Arbor, Mich.: Open Humanities Press, 2016), 7.

75. VanderMeer, *Acceptance*, 105–6.

76. VanderMeer, *Acceptance*, 106.

CONCLUSION

1. Similar to the texts that make up the Southern Reach trilogy, those that make up the overall narrative begun in *Borne* (New York: MCD/Farrar, Straus and Giroux, 2017) are far less complicated in terms of their publication history than are the Veniss or Ambergris texts. Aside from Borne, *The Strange Bird: A Borne Story* (New York: MCD, 2017; initially available only as an unpaginated e-book) is the only other text unquestionably set in this world, although VanderMeer has suggested there may be more to come. Two short stories, "The Third Bear" and "The Situation," both in *The Third Bear*

(San Francisco, Calif.: Tachyon, 2010), describe characters and events closely related to *Borne*. "The Third Bear" describes a village's attempts to stop a bear named "Theeber" or "Seether" (alternative names for the giant bear Mord in *Borne*) from destroying it. In "The Situation," a worker at a strange company, similar to descriptions of the Company in *Borne*, becomes involved with a strange fish project (which also appears, in a rather different form, in *Borne*) and a coworker who transforms into a bear named the Mord (an event also described in *Borne*, albeit in a different form). See also the essay by Jeff VanderMeer, "The Third Bear," in *Monstrous Creatures*, which reproduces some of the short story of the same name and addresses what it is about, namely the need for monsters that do not conform to human standards of what monsters are or should be.

2. VanderMeer, *Borne*, 39.

3. VanderMeer, *Borne*, 166.

4. VanderMeer, *Borne*, 16.

5. Michael D. Shear, "Trump Will Withdraw U.S. from Paris Climate Agreement," *New York Times*, June 1, 2017, https://www.nytimes.com; Oliver Milman, "EPA Head Scott Pruitt Denies that Carbon Dioxide Causes Global Warming," *Guardian*, March 9, 2017, https://www.theguardian.com.

6. Tristram Korten, "In Florida, Officials Ban Term 'Climate Change,'" *Miami Herald*, March 8, 2015, http://www.miamiherald.com.

7. VanderMeer, *Borne*, 268.

8. Steven Shaviro, "Jeff VanderMeer's *Borne*," Pinocchio Theory, April 9, 2017, http://www.shaviro.com/Blog.

9. Jill Owens, "Powell's Interview: Jeff VanderMeer, Author of *Borne*," Powell's, April 7, 2017, http://www.powells.com.

10. Vansanta Studios, *Life in the Broken Places with Jeff VanderMeer*, YouTube (2017), https://www.youtube.com.

11. VanderMeer, *Borne*, 169.

12. VanderMeer, *Borne*, 209.

13. VanderMeer, *Borne*, 297, my emphasis.

14. Clute and Grant, *Encyclopedia of Fantasy*, 458. The terms "healing" and "return" refer to the same part of the grammar of fantasy, but with different inflections. Clute has abandoned the former term and now uses the latter, as in Clute, *Pardon This Intrusion*, 19–31.

15. Clute, *Pardon This Intrusion*, 27. Clute's grammar of science fiction is the least well described of the three (i.e., fantasy, science fiction, and horror). The best description of it is in the essay cited here, although the entries in Clute and Nicholls, *Encyclopedia of Science Fiction*, on "novum" and "conceptual breakthrough" (which he develops into the first and third stages of the grammar) are also helpful, as is Suvin's discussions of the novum and cognitive estrangement (the second stage in the grammar) in *Metamorphoses of Science Fiction*.

16. Clute, *Darkening Garden*, 17.

17. Clute, *Darkening Garden*, 17–18.

18. Jameson, *Archaeologies of the Future*, 288–89.

19. VanderMeer, *Borne*, 241.

20. VanderMeer, *Borne*, 262.

21. VanderMeer, *Borne*, 313.

22. VanderMeer, *Borne*, 279.

23. VanderMeer, *Borne*, 317.

24. VanderMeer, *Borne*, 262.

INDEX

BENJAMIN J. ROBERTSON is assistant professor of English at the University of Colorado, Boulder, and coeditor of *The Johns Hopkins Guide to Digital Media*.

JEFF VANDERMEER was the 2016–17 Trias Writer-in-Residence for Hobart and William Smith Colleges. He is author of the *New York Times* best-selling Southern Reach trilogy (*Annihilation, Authority,* and *Acceptance*), which won the Shirley Jackson Award and the Nebula Award.